Unmatched

SIFRIA PUBLISHING

Unmatched

An Orthodox Jewish woman's mystifying journey to find marriage and meaning

Sarah Lavane

Published by Sifria Publishing

ISBN: 979-8-218-01031-7 (hardcover)
ISBN: 979-8-218-01032-4 (paperback)

Dedicated to my mother, z"l,
the softest shoulder

CONTENTS

PART THREE
How Long Will You Hide Your Countenance (Psalms 13:2)

PART FOUR
I Am with Him in Distress (Psalms 91:15)

Before We Begin...

THIS MEMOIR has been written as a labor of love. My compulsion to share how an Orthodox Jewish single life and its challenges are truly experienced grew over the years. I wanted to clear the air, sweep away presumptions and unlock the door for those who misunderstand. Would sharing my story, just one of thousands, illuminate the layers of complexities? Would it lead to more awareness, compassion, and empathy in those who are "matched" while providing validation and support to the "unmatched"? I didn't know, but I wanted to try. This book in your hand is the result – the key that will open that mystifying door for you.

Won't you step over that threshold and join me? I'll take you along from my early childhood's growing awareness of God and relationships to my adult struggle as I search for a spouse. You'll accompany me on the winding road of adventures, dates, and challenges to my faith. We will arrive at our destination with the lessons I've learned along the way.

Though I've written from my own perspective, these anecdotes describe issues and emotions shared by all. Love, heartbreak, and faith are woven into the fabric of all our lives despite our differing religious outlooks and backgrounds. I included uncomfortable truths regularly brushed aside to avert controversy, yet I sought to disclose those truths with modesty and privacy. As an antidote to the weighty nature of these tales, I relate them with a light touch.

Unlike an autobiography, a memoir focuses on an individual aspect of a person's life. I chose to write about this one challenging sliver. By the same token, any community – in this case, the Orthodox Jewish

1

community – is a rich and multifaceted tapestry of many layers. This book is not meant to be a full reflection of my life nor a study of the community. It covers only those parts, flattering or not, relevant to this story. It would take many more volumes were I to attempt a comprehensive study of this community's contributions, integrity, generosity and unique role among the nations of the world.

While the stories told are true, a memoir is only as true as one's memories. In addition, I've changed details and names to protect identities. As much as I divulge between these covers, there were many more stories that I did not share. I chose those that best reflect the gamut of experiences.

It is impossible to convey the full account, but I hope that by opening the door I have given you a small, yet realistic glimpse into the "unmatched" world.

PART ONE

With All of Your Heart and With All of Your Soul (Deut. 6:5)

בכל לבבך ובכל נפשך (דברים ו:ה)

Language of Love

There were five people in my family and between us, we spoke five different languages. We could have said "I love you" in any of them, but the language of love was tough for us.

My father was Hungarian. He'd point to the platters on the table with his fork and say "Eat. Eat. Take another piece." That was his way of saying *szeretlek*. The rest of us didn't know a word of Hungarian, not even that one, and we could not have pronounced it if we wanted to.

My mother was French-born but she didn't adopt the reckless ideas of love from the French. Her love was measured by her countless selfless acts as a Jewish mother. Nevertheless, on rare occasions, she would sink into the red velvet recliner in the living room, close her eyes and murmur along with Edith Piaf's *La Vie en Rose*. We'd sit and watch the 45rpm spin round and round under the record player's needle in our Brooklyn living room, while our mother seemed to be transported far away. We begged her to teach us some words in her exotic lovely language and she taught us songs such as *Alouette, Gentille Alouette*. We practiced "I love you" in French, *Je t'aime*, in the large ornate mirror above my parents' dresser, along with *bonjour* and *ooh la la* just to roll it around our mouths and pretend we were sophisticated, daring

3

Parisians. When my mother prepared artichoke, we'd really ramp it up. We'd savor – more than the taste – the knowledge that none of our friends' mothers prepared this dish. We'd tilt our invisible berets on our heads, gently dip the petals into oil with our pinkies extended, say the *borei pri ha'adamah* blessing and nibble around the heart. Our exotic French vegetable had a heart. How romantic. Then we'd practice on each other and burst out laughing. *Bon appétit. Ooh la la. Je t'aime! Ha ha, hoo hoo.*

My sister, brother and I were American-born and we learned English in school, but "I love you" would get stuck in our throat like the *ptcha* my mother prepared for our Shabbos meal, that we dare not swallow. My father smacked his lips eating what he considered a European delicacy and my mother pleased him by preparing that gelatinous dish along with all his other favorites – chicken soup and *cholent*. That was her "I love you."

My father would tell us how *geshmak* the dish was while my mother was still pottering around in the kitchen. We'd urge him to tell her, and when she returned to the dining room with another steaming tureen of food, and turned towards him in anticipation, he wouldn't say a thing. So, we'd prod him: "Tatty has something he wants to tell you."

He'd blush like a young boy on a first date and would say "The *ptcha* is…" clearing his throat, "uh… it reminds me of Europe. My mother always made this in Europe." That was his "I love you."

We circled around the words too. We found it easier to say "I love you" by making our parents color-paper cutout birthday cards or tissue-paper flower bouquets that said it for us. Or we'd jump on our parents, wrap our legs around them and burrow our heads in their necks – too shy to meet their eyes and say what we felt. "I love you," felt too intimate. It sounded artificial to us. English was our "outside-the-house" language.

The fourth language in our household was Hebrew. We prayed in Biblical Hebrew, but *Ani ohev otach* was not quoted anywhere in the Bible. Perhaps our forefathers and mothers whispered it in the privacy of their tents. Somehow using the Holy Tongue to talk about our feelings didn't seem appropriate at all – quite blasphemous. This language was strictly for speaking with God.

Finally, our "in-the-house" language was Yiddish. *Ich hob dir lib* sounded guttural and all wrong. Besides, our family spoke Yinglish, a pidgin mixture of Yiddish and English. If we ever dared to say it to each other, we would probably have said "*Ich* love *dir*," which really sounds all wrong.

We had trouble with love in any language.

Earliest Notions of Romance

"Once upon a time," my father would say, "there were twins called the Too Too Twins." On he would go relating bed-time stories of mischief with dire consequences. The Too Too Twins were too loud, too awake, and they did not want to go to sleep. They would jump up and down on their mattresses till the springs creaked, the beds broke, the floor cracked open, and the earth swallowed them all the way to China. They were too, too much trouble. To my father's dismay, his lesson missed the mark. We weren't at all frightened of being swallowed. Instead, my brother, sister and I would eagerly jump harder and higher, whooping and giggling, hoping to visit this strange land where emperors had long, limp ponytails and ladies squished their toes into tiny silk slippers. We bounced till my father's anger made it clear that if we didn't stop prancing around, his "strap" would reach our *tush* before our *tush* landed in any rice paddy. We would quickly recite the *Shema* and snuggle under our covers. When he left the room, I'd jump one more time just to test him. "*Gai shoyn shlufen!*" he'd yell from the kitchen.

My mother, on the other hand, read to us from the bound gilt-edged pages of *Grimm Brothers Fairy Tales* in her soothing voice. The stories of Snow White, Rapunzel, Cinderella, Little Red Riding Hood, Rumpelstiltskin and the rest, enchanted us despite the dwarves, kidnappings, poison, wicked stepsisters, and wolves that kept me awake in fear. I was equally frightened by our biblical ancestral accounts in the *Chumash*. Sarah was kidnapped. Yaakov's bride was switched on him after seven years of labor for her hand in marriage. Yosef was sold into slavery by his brothers.

I was horribly afraid of being kidnapped and worried that my parents would not be able to "afford" the ransom because I used to overhear them talk about what they could and could not "afford." But I did wish for my very own charming *chosson* who would understand me better than anyone else in the entire world, and someday whisk me away. Those stories were probably the beginning of my earliest notions of romance.

As I got older, I'd ask my parents how they met. I didn't realize how unusual it was to have a Hungarian father and a French mother or five spoken languages in one household. Everyone on our street in Brooklyn seemed to be from some faraway land, and I had no idea why or how we all got there. There was a babble of languages, and diverse groups of people: Italians and Irish, Puerto Ricans, Israelis, Indians, and Pakistanis. And a block or two over there were many more of us, observant Jews speaking all sorts of Eastern European languages – Hungarian, Romanian, Czechoslovakian and Polish.

"How did you meet Tatty?" I asked my mother.

"On a blind date." She explained the unexpected call from my father, whose friend she had dated. He had passed her number on to my father.

"But why did you come here to look for a husband? Couldn't you find one in France?" I asked.

"Because I wanted to marry someone who kept Shabbos."

"Weren't there other French Jews like you?"

"There weren't too many of us left after the war." That satisfied my curiosity and inchoate understanding of the war, though I really did not know what it implied.

I didn't know much about war or even which one she referred to. All I knew was that things happened before the war or after the war. My parents lived with their parents before the war. They met and married after the war.

I was clueless as to what my parents' roles were in the war she spoke

6

of or how wars began. As a child, it was just another bewildering thing about the adult world. I thought how lucky we were that there was no war now. If I tacitly understood one thing about war, it was that it was much scarier than any fairy tale.

Honor Your Father and Your Mother

My father was chatting in Hungarian on the phone to his family who lived nearby in Brooklyn. I never understood a word, but sometimes heard our names peppered in his staccato-sounding speech, and I'd wonder what he was saying about us. My mother, on the other hand, rarely spoke to our grandfather who lived in Paris. Long distance phone calls in the 1970s were prohibitively expensive. So, we would find aerograms edged in blue and red on the hallway floor, under the mail slot on the door. We'd happily grab it and race up the stairs to our apartment to deliver this precious bounty to her, knowing it would please her.

My mother would sit down at the kitchen table in her duster and tuck her loose hair back under her kerchief, carefully slice the aerogram open with a knife, push her glasses up her nose and start to read. Whether she was reading those mysterious scripted words or was on one of her rare calls, we'd gather around her, pleased for her, and watch her brown eyes light up and her pale skin blush. On the calls, she'd be bonjour-ing, oo-la-la-ing, and bonsoir-ing much better than we did at her mirror.

One day, it dawned on me there was no Yiddish on my parents' calls.

"Mommy if you speak French to your family and Tatty speaks Hungarian to his, how did either of you know Yiddish?"

"We didn't speak Yiddish very well either, but better than English." That gave me pause. *How did my parents communicate when they met?*

One summer, when I was a teenager, we visited cousins in Israel. They were fluent in Hebrew and French, while my siblings and I were fluent in Yiddish and English. It was then that I realized how much one can convey without speaking a common language. We motioned a lot with our hands and faces and spoke louder, as though that would help. Mostly, we played with each other and "play" is a universal language. Somehow, we understood each other. Somewhat.

I also realized that when I prayed from my prayer book in Hebrew, I did not know what all the words meant, but I understood the gist of what I was saying. We were either praising God – why He would need little girls in Brooklyn praising Him was beyond me. We were begging Him for favors, and God knows we needed plenty of those. Lastly, we were thanking Him for everything because it's only right and polite to thank Him for everything we had. My speaking-Hebrew vocabulary was a far cry from my reading-Hebrew, yet I fervently spoke to God in Hebrew every day, even though I didn't understand half of what I was saying.

Odd.

We spoke Yiddish at home, a dialect of German, even though neither of my parents spoke it in their homes, neither were German-born and the Germans were the bad guys in the vague "war" I still knew little about.

Odder still.

It may not make much sense, but it was our normal. When our ancestors received the Torah on Mount Sinai, they proclaimed "Na'ase v'nishma" – "We will do, and we will hear." The Jewish way is to jump in and do the *mitzvos* and say the prayers. In that way, we will come to understand them better.

I asked my mother about their dates.

"We went out for coffee or walks. There were just one or two kosher restaurants in New York back in those days." I urged her to tell me more. "One day, I slipped on ice and fell into a snowbank. Tatty rescued me."

Ah... my parents had romantic moments. I couldn't imagine them that way. Throughout their marriage, my parents' cultural differences were always present. My father was a boy who went to *cheder* in a small Eastern European town, while my mother had attended public school in a non-Jewish suburb as well as *Talmud Torah* in Paris' famous *pletzl* in the Marais district. My father was loud and gregarious on the phone, my mother quiet, shy, and busy in the kitchen. But I was glad to hear that my father rescued my mother from the snow.

Often as a grown woman when I'd sit across a restaurant table from a gentleman, I'd find we'd both stare at our menus or our plates because we didn't understand each other at all, even though we spoke the same language. So much for sharing a language.

My parents were both Sabbath-observing Jews and yet they seemed like an intermarriage of sorts – a Western European married to an Eastern European. One day it occurred to me that if not for those very evil Germans I'd heard whispers about, my parents would never have moved to America and would never have met and would never have had me.

So, there you go. My mind had braided up a thought-pretzel.

The Germans were very bad, but if not for them, I would not have been born. My mother would be living in Paris with a French husband, smearing butter on her baguettes and croissants and my father would've married a local town girl who'd sprinkle paprika on his goulash. None of us would be on American soil speaking English.

But pretzel is a German word, is it not?

Snips and Snails and Puppy Dog Tails

I went to an all-girls *yeshiva* where the only men were the administrators or the janitors. They all seemed serious or busy to me, except for the principal, Rabbi SmilingEyes, whose smile pierced his long silver beard and who always said hello with a twinkle in his eye.

I was not completely shielded and separated from boys. There was my brother, close in age to me, who many assumed was my twin when we were young. He had his own blue room at the front of the apartment while I shared a pink room in the back with my sister. I'd double check the door locks before going to bed. I didn't want any intruder sneaking in and carting him off in his pajamas while the rest of us slept unawares, especially as he was the only brother I had, and a very good one.

9

There were the boys in our summer bungalow colony in the Catskill Mountains, who competed to see whose swing would fly higher or who could swat the most flies. There were my boy cousins, one of whom, Bear, used to tell us ghost stories under the big oak tree. There was the caretaker, Old Joe, whose tremors scared us. Bear told us that Old Joe was bitten by a rabid dog, which cemented my fear of dogs for years to come.

In the city, there were other boys – my brother's yeshiva friends, and our neighbor, who played Monopoly with my brother, while my sister and I played with his sisters. There was a schoolyard across the street, but it was full of bullies, so we mostly played in front of our own house and watched the drama from our side of the street or our second-floor porch.

A Puerto Rican boy, Luis, whose father was the super of a nearby building, aimed to run me over with his bike. My Italian upstairs neighbor, Gianni, a few years older and a lot beefier than us scrawny Jewish kids, would come to the rescue and threaten to beat Luis up. "These kids do anything to you, huh Luis? 'Cuz I sure will, if you don't scram!"

One day, my mother recruited Gianni to teach me how to ride my bike. I skipped after him to the schoolyard with the prettiest bubblegum pink bicycle in the whole wide world. I was eager to try it. My mother watched from the porch. I waved to her. Gianni held the back of the white banana seat as I climbed on and told me to pedal.

"I won't let go," he promised. "Pedal faster!" he commanded as he ran along with me and my bike. With Gianni there, I felt secure and the bike went very fast. I turned around to smile at him but he was no longer there – he had let go! I was on my own. The shock threw me off balance and I promptly fell and bloodied my knee, but from then on, I knew how to ride my bike. I had a silent and distant crush on Gianni, but knew he wasn't "one of us," so the possibility of me cycling off into the sunset with him was as remote as Prince Charming showing up at my door with a horse-drawn carriage.

School Rules

My school had a lot of strict rules. We could not own a TV. The sign forbidding it was right in the lobby. As we had a TV, this caused me much anxiety because every day I was breaking a rule. I'd push open the glass doors and creep right past that sign, imagining that one of the principals with x-ray vision would somehow know and throw me out.

Even as a child, I wondered why the school didn't bring up the matter with the parents instead of scaring the girls with that sign in the lobby. I would come home so nervous and loaded up with so much homework that took me hours to finish after a long day at school with a Hebrew and English double curriculum. The only thing to relieve my anxiety was to watch *I Love Lucy* or some other show that would make me laugh, which in turn created more anxiety about breaking the rule.

Another school rule was that we couldn't talk to boys. If we went to the pizza shop on our way home from school on Fridays, we were forbidden to talk to boys. If we went for a walk on Shabbos afternoon, we were forbidden to flirt with the boys. There wasn't much we could do Shabbos afternoons. We could study the *parshah*, read, and go for walks. We had *Bnos* groups where my friends and I played games, danced, or learned songs. But we could not do our homework, watch TV, draw, play our melodica, trade our stationery, or do our needlepoints. Why was it a big deal if some girls talked to some boys? That would be normal socialization for most kids.

I didn't understand why we were forbidden, for as a young child I did not understand the way girls in the "outside world" could "get into trouble" with boys. I was an obedient child, a good student, and aside from the TV rule, I was not a rule-breaker. We had school six days a week and so much homework there really was no time for any mischief. On Fridays, we'd get out early, I'd stop for pizza, do errands for my mother and have a long walk home.

I had no time or interest in boys, but the rule nevertheless irritated me. Why did the school tell us what we could do on our off-hours when we had so few of them? We were not like the wild kids in the

11

schoolyard across the street from my home. We didn't dress like them, talk like them, nor behave like them. Even Gianni and his siblings were not like those kids. So why did we need that rule?

One day we came to school and learned that our classmate, Flirt, had gotten into big trouble. She had been caught talking to a boy on Shabbos. And worse, she had flirted in full view of passersby. She was in danger of getting suspended. Was it unseemly behavior in their eyes? *If only they saw what I see in the schoolyard!* Flirting was nothing.

Though I befriended Gianni and his brother Nicky, I was still a very conscientious girl who prayed daily and got good grades. I was glad to have some exposure to people with different views and lifestyles than my own, for it gave me a window to the world outside. Even with my front row seat at the schoolyard theater, I never saw what happened behind closed doors. If I had, I still would not imagine any of that happening to any of my classmates. The world on the other side of the street, was indeed another planet that none of us were part of. Seeing bits and pieces of that world in the yard and on TV helped me intuitively understand how my own lifestyle as a Jewish child – with difficult rules for everything – was working in my favor like a red traffic light that prevents one from crashing. I chafed at the myriad school rules, but I thanked God for the red lights.

The Kohen Gadol and The Fiddler

Every Monday morning in seventh grade, my teacher would chalk a verse across the top of the blackboard that remained there all week. Sometimes it was a verse from the Torah, Talmud, or *Chazal* – a lesson-of-the-week theme. One time she wrote the Mishnah, "Do not be sure of yourself. For Yochanan the High Priest, served as *Kohen Gadol* for eighty years and in the end, he became a Sadducee." This teacher gave me stomach cramps. In her efforts to control the class, she was strict, spoke so quietly we had to strain to hear her, and gave us hours' worth of homework each day. She also spoke so rapidly that we had to race to write pages and pages of notes. When I wrote my notes in Yiddish,

12

from right to left, my hand would slide over the fresh ink of words just written and turn blue. This was true of all classes, but in her class, my hands turned as blue as my mood. The only verse I recall from ten months of school verses on the blackboard was this one. It frightened me. How could a man who was a *Kohen Gadol* for eighty years go bad like a rotten tomato? What happened to him? She never told us. She did however warn us we had to be vigilant in our observance because if we weren't, we could slide off into nowhere. *Could we?* The only place I had seen this happen was in a Hollywood film.

In *Fiddler on the Roof,* Tevye the milkman's daughters sing the lyrics "Matchmaker, matchmaker, make me a match, find me a find, catch me a catch" in their plea to Yente the matchmaker, to find them good husbands. One by one, the older daughters get married. I evaluated all their choices and wondered if I would marry them. Yente proposes Lazer the town's prosperous butcher. He's a much older, heavy-set widower and fortunately is cast aside after a ghostly nightmare. *Whew! What a relief.* Instead, the eldest daughter, Tzeitel, marries the good-hearted Motel the tailor. He whirls her around singing about the miraculous turn of events. *Nice guy but seems too goofy and simple for me.*

The next daughter, Hodel marries Perchik, the revolutionary Jew who rejects tradition. He is arrested and exiled to Siberia, where Hodel, clad in heavy shawls, follows him. *He has more fire and spark, but he's a worrisome character. And Siberia? Really? I'll pass. The idea of it chills my bones.*

The third daughter is studious Chava, who meets Fyedka, the handsome gentile who protects her from the other taunting boys, as Gianni had done for me. He loans her a book. They secretly fall in love – *God have mercy – a Christian* – and when they decide to marry, her father understandably won't hear of it and so she elopes. I cry for Chava's choice. Apparently Tzeitel and Motel are the happiest match, and even have a baby before they're all chased out of Anatevka by order of the czar. The movie broke my heart. Do people leave their Jewish values for love? For ideas? For beliefs? Are Jews expelled from their homes for those same values?

I shuddered at losing my home and knew that both my parents had been forced to leave theirs. *Could that happen to me, too?* More than that, I asked myself, if faced with a choice between a fat old butcher or the handsome, young, non-Jewish intellectual, would I pick either of them? Would I stay alone? I think back to that blackboard verse and Yochanan the *Kohen Gadol*. Chava was young and carried away by her passion, but Yochanan was a High Priest in his old age! *What were his reasons for leaving the fold? What could they be?* I shuddered.

Warning Bells

I was not a class star in school, but I wasn't a wallflower. I wasn't a goody two-shoes, but neither was I the class clown or troublemaker.

I was an earnest student, that teachers for the most part appreciated. I walked to school with my friends and played with them at recess.

But I was not a conformist. Perhaps because I lived further away from the school. Perhaps because I played with all my neighbors – Jewish and not. Perhaps because my mother was a Western European, not a provincial Eastern-European or American-born.

My high school taught us Regents subjects and we could take the SATs, however they encouraged us to go to seminary for a year after high school and to marry. The joke was that seminary was just a way to guarantee an MRS. degree.

I preferred to go to college instead. I wanted to figure out what to do with my future. This was one of the many times I regretted not having switched to a religious high school more in line with my *hashkafah* – a school that would support my efforts. I went to the office of the principal, Rabbi Warner, to get my transcript so I could apply for college. They were painting his office walls and his desk was piled with papers and boxes. He looked distracted, but between talking to the contractors and answering his phone, he managed to warn me of the dangers of public college.

"You realize the dangers of going to college?" he asked. "The way they'll influence you?" *If high school hasn't managed to influence me, college won't either. I wouldn't marry at nineteen, but I won't run off like Chava in* "Fiddler on the Roof."

There were Jewish colleges, but they were prohibitively expensive. I understood academia was liberal and I was not, but I would attend night school after work and go home from there. I would not get involved in campus life and would live at home. As I had grown up with non-Jewish neighbors and survived religiously intact, I did not fear the influence of college. I remembered my seventh-grade teacher's warning, but I was sincerely pious and strong in my faith. I did not want to attend seminary, but I resolved to study Jewish texts weekly. The night classes would be full of observant Jews like me. Rabbi Warner was worried enough to warn me, but more concerned about his office being painted. The school bell rang. He handed over my transcript.

Child Brides and the Domino Effect

During our senior year, a Sephardic classmate became engaged to be married just months before graduation. She was seventeen, and I was flabbergasted. In Yemen, where her parents came from, girls married young, so seventeen was practically an old maid. By that time, between the schoolyard, the TV, the library, and some heartfelt talks I had with my mother, I was aware of the facts of life, but wondered whether all the sheltered girls in my class were as well.

Some of my classmates were Chassidic, had no TV, no non-Jewish neighbors, nor mothers to whom they could talk as openly as I could to mine. *What did they know?* So in hushed discussions with some of my friends, I discovered some knew more than I expected them to – by osmosis, through the Chassidic grapevine or their more modern classmates like me.

I wondered if Sephardic would return to school as a married "woman" to finish twelfth grade and get her diploma. I was completely mystified by this rush to get married and not finish school. Would she experience a fantasy wedding with lace and silk swishing, her diamond flashing, her dazzling white teeth smiling, the food, the music, the flowers, the veil all swirling together, leading to a night she had always dreamed of or a night she never expected? Would it be her short moment in the spotlight, leading to a life of regrets, or a marriage that bound two kindred young souls on their journey into mature adulthood?

I didn't think marrying young was terrible or any more prone to failure than getting married when older. I did think giving up one's diploma just one month shy of earning it was not prudent. It seemed to me that some girls thought of the diamond rings and bridal gowns and all the wedding details but did not think much of their actual marriage. I was only a teenager, but I was still the philosopher I had been as a child.

Sephardic did not show up for our graduation and did not finish school. The following year, many more of my classmates were engaged. Some of them were more modern and had dated their new spouses over months. The Chassidic girls for the most part met in someone's living room, after their families had thoroughly vetted each suitor. These were not arranged marriages, but they were arranged dates. No one was forced to marry someone she didn't like, but I imagined some may have felt peer, social, or family pressure to agree, even when doubtful or unsure. Those engaged to the first man they met joked about checking out more apartments or gowns than men. I didn't see the humor in that.

Most would likely attend *kallah* classes, private sessions that taught them the *halachos* of family purity. Those who didn't know much, would find out. Perhaps they were groomed for this, and I was the naive one, but I was troubled that some would commit to marriage before fully comprehending a major part of it.

I had spent the last four years of life with schoolwork, some hobbies, and not much else. I had a solid education in my Jewish and secular studies, but I had not experienced much. I dislike the cliche of "wanting to find oneself," but I suppose that's exactly what I needed. I craved companionship but did not feel ready for marriage. *Why did so few others seem to feel the way I did?*

If my friends and I could be compared to the March sisters of *Little Women*, I suppose I'd fit into Jo's role best. Jo didn't quite fit in. She was a bit ambitious and independent. My friends resembled Meg, Beth and Amy more. They were beautiful, pious, had more social graces. When pressed, "Amy" confided that she looked forward to the privacy and one-on-one interaction as part of a couple rather than being a sister lost in a crowd of siblings.

Girls barely out of their teens were panicked or distraught at not being married. Aside from a desire for companionship, societal, and peer pressure affected my classmates more so than in other religious circles. They were like a line of dominoes pushing each other. As soon as one got engaged, another seemed to follow. Bam. Bam. Bam. Bam. It was the year of weddings.

Fortunately, I didn't feel the pressure at nineteen and wasn't as frantic as the others. Some girls were depressed if they were not married at age twenty. Every now and then, when someone married at twenty-five, she would be lamented for "marrying late" as though she were forty-five. I thought this attitude served to reinforce despair rather than offer hope to those still looking.

I had faith that my turn would come at the right time for me and that God would help me.

Butterflies

At twenty years old, I worked as a typesetter and mechanical paste-up artist during the daytime and attended college for computer science at night. It was exhausting but exhilarating. This schedule seemed lighter than my high school curriculum, as I took only two classes at night. I had considerably less homework as well as free Sundays. My lunch break consisted of wandering the winding canyon streets of the Wall Street area and drinking it all in – the ships and shops at the South Street Seaport; the discovery of a real fort at Battery Park; the modern-day Towers of Babel – the World Trade Center Twin Towers that seemed to reach the heavens. I loved exploring and learning.

Between evening classes and after them, I attended wedding after wedding. Most of my classmates did not go to college, though some would continue their schooling years later. I wanted to get married and have kids. I wanted companionship and love, but I also wanted a bit more time before getting married. Only a bit. I especially wanted my older sister to find her mate first. I didn't want to beat her to the *chuppah* or pain her in any way. Though she encouraged me to start dating, I still hoped she'd meet someone before I did.

I met men in college – both eligible men and not, but mostly not. The boys who shared my background seem to shy away from saying hello or did not seem to notice me. They were in cliques with their sisters' friends and others. So, I talked to the boys who did notice me.

In a summer speech class, there was Pat. He was tall, Irish, redheaded, and built like a football player. His eyes twinkled when he laughed and he always seemed to be laughing. There were also four Sabbath-observant men in my class. We were acutely aware of each other with our internal laser, and even when they did not really look my way, I knew they knew I was there. We were like family in a foreign country. One serious boy nodded when I passed him in the hallway. The other three averted my gaze as though they did not notice me.

The teacher formed us into groups for study sessions, and Pat was in mine. He was very charming, and off-limits, of course. But all the other girls vied for his attention.

"Do you have a pen for me, Pat?" One woman's hand goes on his arm.

"You're so funny and adorable!" Another's lashes flutter at him over her shoulder.

"Do you like my new outfit?" A third twines her hair between her fingers.

I'd seen it all before in the schoolyard. I did like Pat, even had butterflies in my stomach when I was near him, but I couldn't and wouldn't play this game. I rolled my eyes at it all and then caught Pat rolling his eyes too and smiling at me – at the shared reaction. Without intending to, it was I and my reticence, which drew his attention.

After class, Pat and I strolled to the bus stop together. We always had interesting discussions, but I did not flutter my lashes, nor twirl my hair. I wished I could have these nice talks with one of the four Jewish men and worried what they thought when they saw my easy camaraderie with this non-Jew. *Did they think I was a black sheep, a lost cause?* They weren't talking to me at all, and Pat was.

One day I came into class late and was about to sit down when Pat whispered and pointed at my chair, "There's a bug!"

I gratefully found another seat and after that, sweet bug jokes between us began. Summer session was nightly, so we saw each other night after night. He offered me his jacket when I shivered. He told me his dream was to someday be a podiatrist, but I envisioned him as a friendly big Irish firefighter.

On the last day of classes, the women were all throwing themselves into his arms. My heart twinged as I watched them all.

I could never reach the levels of our *Imahos*, but I resolved to be like Rebecca in *Ivanhoe* or Mirah in *Daniel Deronda*. I was moved to think the gentile authors of these classics must have modeled their characters after Jewish women they had encountered in real life – women whose devotion to their faith had impressed them. I could aim to be an ordinary Jewish woman like these nameless women. I was young and dramatic. If viewing myself as a heroine devoted to her faith, helped me do the right thing, so be it.

He waited for me to walk to the bus stop together one last time and I admitted to him that I will miss him. He said we can stay in touch. I knew it wouldn't be good for me, so I told him I am an observant Jew, assuming he will understand my coolness. "Well, someday I'll be a podiatrist. You can always look me up." I said I would and meant it. We wished each other the best and continued walking in silence, aware of every moment slipping away with each step.

As we neared the stop, I saw one of our buses approaching but did not know whose it was. We raced toward it and I panicked. How would I say an abrupt goodbye? I did not want to. We both ran to the door till

19

we saw it was his bus. Pat turned to me and exclaimed, "There's a bug!" while pointing to my chest.

I looked down in alarm. He quickly stole a kiss on my cheek and leapt onto the bus.

My cheek was aflame, branded.

I saw his green eyes sparkling with mischief on the bus. The last bug joke was on me.

He waved, and the bus disappeared down the road while I stood there, stunned. My hand rose to cup my cheek. I could smell his manly aroma. I could feel the scratchy tug on my skin. I could sense his love and respect. My hand stayed there, trying to preserve those new sensations, trying to hold on to that kiss for posterity. Like a beautiful butterfly, I never wanted to let it go, but eventually it fluttered away.

Years later, I needed a podiatrist and looked up Pat. He had indeed fulfilled his dream. His face had weathered nicely and he had married. Despite all that had transpired since we last met, he was as warm and friendly as ever and his eyes still twinkled when he laughed.

Blindsided

My cousin called me to say he had a blind date suggestion. I had begun to meet with matchmakers, but I had more confidence when acquaintances suggested a date. Then my cousin told me this person had been in my class during the summer and had been impressed with me. I had been sure that those four yeshiva boys had disapproved of my friendship with Pat, and now one of them wanted to meet me?

I thought it must be the guy who occasionally acknowledged me with his nod. My cousin told me that Nodder asked around about me until he found our family connection. On one hand, I felt flattered that he went through all that trouble to track down someone who knew me. On the other hand, wasn't that silly when I was right there for the asking? So, he pursued me, but in a round-about fashion. Okay. I'll try it. Perhaps he did not wish to put me on the spot.

Was I really the kind of person Nodder would want to marry? I could hear my high school principal's voice warning me about college. I did not want to marry a "Pat," I wanted to marry a religious man. I agreed to the date.

Nodder rang the bell. I opened the door and the man standing there was definitely not Nodder. He was one of the other three who never even glanced my way! During dinner, I said, "I thought I made a bad impression by always talking to Pat."

"Not at all! You were so nice and outgoing, I thought that's the kind of girl I want to marry."

It was a pleasant surprise to hear that. Trouble was that I, too, wanted to marry someone nice and outgoing. Not-Nodder was nice, but he wasn't outgoing. He didn't speak to me at all in that class. We went out several more times, partly to make sure, and partly because he was my first date and he kept asking me out. I had no experience at rejecting someone. So, I kept saying "yes" and kept thinking, *next time I have to say "no."* I could tell he was a "fine boy" as the matchmakers would say about many of the "boys," but Not-Nodder was not the right one for me.

In my quest to expand my social circles, I applied to work with a coed *kiruv* group for kids. I had gone to a camp where religious girls did *kiruv* with some irreligious campers. I thought it would also be a nice atmosphere in which to meet young men with my values. The interviewer didn't account for the fact that I had taken the initiative to contact him. He didn't ask why I was interested or whether I had ever done it before. He glanced at my application, saw the school I had gone to and said, "Oh, you would never know how to interact with public school kids," even though I had done so almost my entire life. This effort to expand my opportunities to meet compatible men failed.

My mother dragged me to *shadchanim* – matchmakers. I filled out forms and answered very personal questions. Everything from what my father did for a living – he was a sample maker in the fashion industry – to whether I had gone to seminary – no – and more. I didn't have much faith in this process because I knew most of my answers were not the "good" answers they were looking for. I thought back to Yente and Lazer the Butcher and prayed, *God, in the merit of walking away from Pat, please bring the right one to me.*

Instead, the men who showed up had different names and different jobs, but my next few dates were all Lazer-the-Butchers. I did not know why a matchmaker would set me up with men old enough to have fathered me.

I was aggravated to waste both my time and theirs, as well as their money, but what I dreaded most was to be seen in public with them. I did not want the waiter or the other patrons to think I was "with" this person. I wanted a sign on my back saying "I'm not with him. This is an awful blind date."

Despite my mortification, I tried hard to be as gracious as I could while with someone. If we were not a match, it was not the "Lazer's" fault, it was the "Yente's" fault, and every human being deserves to be treated the way I'd want to be treated. The problem with that, as I learned soon enough, is that the Lazers often wanted a second date. This was not going to be easy. To think I had worried that I'd meet someone before I was ready for marriage. Now I began to fear the opposite would be true.

Two Rendezvous

Sometimes perceptions got in the way — my own as well as others'. As a Computer Science major in Brooklyn College, I had access to a messaging system for all computer science students in the entire CUNY system. This was pre-internet and email days, so it was exciting to be able to converse with others this way. Our monitors were hooked up to modems that cradled our phones.

Somehow, religious Jewish Computer Science majors in the five boroughs of New York City found each other. A few observant students from Riverdale and Staten Island flirted with me, the Brooklyn girl. Reaching someone from another borough felt like a transatlantic communication in the 1980s. I was thrilled to be expanding my social network.

One yeshiva guy seemed like me – observant, but open and engaged in the world. He wasn't averse to speaking with me – or rather, typing to me. We typed and clacked on our keyboards till late. My father would come out of his bedroom, complaining "Why are you click-clacking at this hour? How will you get up for work tomorrow?"

There was another student who was more modern. He had gone to a coed school. It was thrilling to connect with those outside my usual circles and find common ground.

Over time, YeshivaGuy, told me he couldn't wait to meet me and that he would like to date me as soon as he graduated college. I felt the same. Right now, we were both overloaded with work, yeshiva, and school. He was definitely no Lazer-the-Butcher. Soon the click-clacking increased, along with my father's yelling. Our feelings spilled over the keyboard into real mail. I'd study his handwriting and smell the envelope. I fell in love with the curves of his script. My heart leapt at the sight of another letter from him. Now it was my mother's turn to grow concerned when she saw the volume of mail. "You haven't met him, why are you writing so much to each other?"

A great deal of what he said resonated with me and I could not wait to meet him. I wondered what he'd look like and whether I would be as attracted to him as I was to his handwriting and his words.

In the meantime, CoedGuy was intrigued by me. He had dated throughout high school, and here I was from an all-girls school. His impression of me was that I was sheltered and never spoke to boys, and he prided himself, incorrectly, on being the first to break through the barrier. It amused me to see how wrong he was. I was, after all, pining for YeshivaGuy not CoedGuy.

CoedGuy invited me to participate in a *Shabbaton* that welcomed unaffiliated Jews and taught them about Judaism. It was a place where everyone – male and female, religious and non-religious – would spend Shabbos together. That was exactly the sort of weekend I was interested in going to, and was about to tell him so, but had a better idea. His tone suggested that my background and schooling would disapprove of this weekend, but I knew that he would introduce me to a whole new world if I were brave enough to show up. His assumptions irritated me. My school would have definitely disapproved, that part was true, but hadn't he figured out by now that I was not cut from the same cloth? If I shared that frame of mind, would I have so easily conversed with him online?

I decided to feed into his impression of me as the helpless, confined, strict damsel he thought I was. I typed my message:

—*I'd love to go but I have to think about it. It's coed, after all. Not my thing.*

—*You should break out of your narrow circles and come. I'll take care of you. Don't be shy.*

He would be my personal hero. Grr!!

—*My father would not stand for this*, I typed. This was untrue. It just fit CoedGuy's narrative so neatly.

—*Why? Does he only want you to meet men through matchmakers?*

The truth was that my father wanted me to get married, by hook or by crook; and if I met someone acceptable on my own, he would happily pay for a wedding and invite every one of his friends.

—*That's exactly right. I'm sorry but I can't go.*

—*That's too bad. Really. I kinda wanted to meet you. You sound more open-minded than your kind.*

My kind? Really now!

—*I'm not that sort of a girl!!!!* I typed back clicking furiously, indignantly, as though meeting people at a religious retreat was an immoral thing to do and a preposterous idea. His assumptions infuriated me! It was easy for me to play this indignant role.

I was the opposite of shy and helpless. I had already broken the mold by confronting my principal, and by attending a public college. I would show up at the *Shabbaton* not knowing a soul, and not warning him in advance. I would shatter his misconceptions.

Weeks later, I entered the synagogue giddy with excitement about meeting CoedGuy. I had no idea what he would look like. Scanning the room, I spotted a tall young man with a crocheted *kippah* with CoedGuy's name bordering it, speaking to a young lady. Still uncertain, I called out his name, he turned when he heard it, but did not know who called him. His face seemed to match the personality I knew. I called out his name again and he took a step closer. His eyebrows lifted. He chewed his lip as it dawned on him who I might be. He broke into a smile.

"You're here!" he exclaimed. The girl he was speaking to, NYGirl, turned towards me. "That's great! You had me believe you were … oh, never mind. Wow! I can't believe you're here! Let me introduce you to some of my friends." He started with NYGirl, then they guided me into the milling crowd. Everyone was welcoming and warm and made me feel included. Friday night he walked me back to my host family's home. We sat on their porch and talked late into the night. He was so different from the Lazer-the-Butchers I'd been meeting on blind dates. But he seemed so far out of my league that I didn't consider him a possibility for myself.

Nevertheless, I embraced the friendship and became a member of this group. NYGirl and some of the other women quickly became a major part of my college world. I started attending many of their parties and get-togethers because it was inspiring to see so many unaffiliated Jews become religious and hear the stories of their journeys. These *Shabbatonim* uplifted me spiritually and strengthened my faith. It was a kosher environment, led by a rabbi, in which to meet sincere men and women who cared about Judaism. I was happy to make new friends who aligned with my values.

CoedGuy was charismatic, but I had been writing to YeshivaGuy for months and felt we were a more realistic match. I had skipped seminary and he had skipped his yeshiva year in Israel, yet we were both entrenched in Judaism. Our family backgrounds were similar and we had shared so many secrets over the year through our letters.

Finally, as both of us were attending a flurry of weddings, we discovered we'd both be at the same one. This was it. We would finally meet "unofficially" and then after graduation we planned to date "officially." We both felt eager to date but also felt too young. We were aligned even on that.

The excitement was more than I could bear. I would wear a silky dress I had sewn. I would wear heels and iridescent nail polish which I had only begun wearing not too long ago, after high school. I would do my hair and makeup, and I would finally feel like a young lady. *This will be the most exciting night of my life. To think I would meet him at a wedding of all places! Then, we'll probably get married and have lots of babies… and his last name sounds so great with mine…and, and, and…* I was getting carried away.

My mother interrupted my thoughts, "You haven't even met him yet, young lady. You wrote too many letters to him. I don't want you to get hurt." Getting hurt was not a possibility in my book. He opened his heart to me and he was so honest with me. *No way.*

The day of the wedding arrived and we agreed to meet in the large foyer of the reception hall. I told him my dress would be sky blue with a big bow. He would be wearing a black hat and a gray suit. So of course, he'd spot me first. I was standing alone, holding my clutch, fixing my hair, wondering from which direction he'd appear. Then the sea of suits parted and there he was. I knew it was him, from the way he was looking at me. He had a thin face and his black bangs were swept to the side. He was not what I had imagined, but he was my beloved pen pal.

We hit it off right at the start. His voice was so distinctive and matched his handwriting. It was easy to be with him and it all felt so right. I could tell he was as giddy as I was. We planned to continue our correspondence and to start dating when we both graduated. I came home on a cloud. My mother was wrong. Everything was perfect.

As graduation approached, I was looking forward to having free time and dating YeshivaGuy. Since the wedding, we had been speaking on the phone. Then one day, he called and delivered the news that would delay our plans. "I've decided to go study in Israel for a year."

"You what?" I could not believe what I was hearing.

"I never went after high school…"

"Neither did I…"

"…and if I'm ever going to do it, it has to be now."

"A year? Now?"

"If you're still single when I return, we could date, but I wouldn't want to hold you back from meeting other guys. I want you to move on."

"Other guys? Move on?" *After all the shared messages, heartfelt letter writing, complimentary calls and endless, hopeful and serious anticipation of dating for marriage, he was leaving?*

"You there?" he asked.

I was sick to my stomach. The anticipation had built up and now he had burst my balloon, big time. *But what was a year? It will fly by!* I had invested too much in him to let it go to waste.

"I'm here and I'll be here when you return. We could write letters again," I said. Calls to Israel were too expensive.

"We could, but I don't think it's wise. I think it's better if you date other people."

Other people? What was he talking about? Was he no longer interested in me? Did he doubt that our connection could stay strong over a year apart?

I didn't doubt it. We had already waited. I would wait again. But to soothe him, I gave him my word that I would be open to meeting others. I believed he felt bad about leaving, but I did not believe he had lost interest. I promised myself that when he returned, I would be ready and waiting. He promised me he'd call upon his return.

I had a year-long calendar on a narrow strip of paper that spanned the length of my keyboard at work, and I scotch-taped it right beneath the keyboard. Every day, I'd cross off the tiny date and know I was a day closer to his return. I was heartbroken, but in the meantime, I pushed myself to go on.

Heartsick

One of the saddest experiences I've had dating was Stricken. I noticed him at a party. It was hard to miss him beneath the colored streamers. He was stick thin and wearing a wig. His glasses seemed to fill out his shrunken face. I wondered what the matter was. People seemed to know him from school and he joined in the conversations easily. He ambled over and started making small talk. After a few moments, he had put me at ease and I could put aside what he looked like. Then the unexpected happened.

"Would you like to go out?" he asked. Zoom. Suddenly his skeletal appearance and his wig boomeranged right back into view. No one had ever met me at a party and asked me out on the spot. I was flattered, but caught unawares. I couldn't think straight and said "Yes."

I could not sleep that night. As I tossed and turned and fought with my blanket, I had more time to think. *Was I a shallow person who did not want to be seen in public with Stricken? Would I be thrilled to date him if he were not sick? Would Stricken give me a chance, or be remotely interested in me if he were not ill and other girls did not turn him down? Would he be fairer to me than other men had been? The men who judged me by where I lived, what school I had attended, my parents' lack of degrees and professional credentials or the fact that I was first generation American?*

I did not know, but I re-evaluated. He was clearly smart, confident, and probably incredibly cute when he wasn't ill. God was giving me a chance. In this cut-throat dating scene where men had lists of women waiting for a chance to date them, God had sent a man who didn't have a list. I was at the top of his list. This was an opportunity. I would look forward to this date.

Stricken picked me up and started driving. I was glad we were both facing the road because he had seemed shockingly weak and gaunt at the door. He had looked at me with hunger in his eyes – the look a man has when he sees a beautiful woman out of his reach. I was not accustomed to being looked at that way. It frightened me.

At the restaurant, he again tried to put me at ease. But this was different from the party where everyone knew him. We were in a public restaurant, where every waiter suddenly appeared incredibly hale, hearty, and handsome in comparison, where the couples at the other tables turned to stare, where I was clearly struggling against the shallowness in my mind. Perhaps I was not mature enough to handle this. He was created in the image of God and he was a good, good person. Why God had afflicted him with this illness was hard to understand. It weighed on me. We hadn't addressed it at all.

"Um… there's something I…"

"It's okay," he knew where I was going with this, "it's cancer – but I am a fighter and I plan on beating this thing." He slapped the table as though it were the "thing."

He told me about the big rabbi he had gone to for a blessing, who had gifted him a silver *Kiddush* cup with a blessing for a long and healthy life.

He looked at me, "I'm determined to get married and use this *Kiddush* cup at my *chuppah*."

Oh my, oh my, oh my. My heart raced. *Had he set his heart on marrying me?* I studied the stain on the tablecloth. I could not meet his eyes. I wanted to go home and cry.

Later at home, I cried to my mother about illness and choices and what-do-I-dos? I prayed to God, "Please help me navigate this. Tell me what to do." I could barely last through that one dining experience, how could I date or marry him? What if he died, God forbid? I'd be a young widow. I was a mess after one date, what would happen if I continued to date him?

If I rejected him, would it hurt him after one date as much as YeshivaGuy's semi-rejection after months, had hurt me? *Yes*, I thought, *it would*. Should I continue to see him because I felt too sorry to reject him? He would not want that. This was going to be painful one way or another. I could not handle it. I was a complete and utter wreck.

He called and chatted about his plans for our next date. My stomach was lurching, but I had to stop this right away. I did not want to give him false hope for another moment. I interrupted him. "There's something I need to speak to you about." He was quiet. He knew what was coming. I felt dreadful.

"Don't bother," he spat back, "you think I don't know what you're gonna tell me? You think I haven't heard it before?" His tone shocked me. He had been so amiable and solicitous until now. I had expected hurt, shock, or sadness, but not this poisonous anger.

"People who look like you don't have to worry about getting married like I do." People who *look like me?* Some men considered me attractive while others did not, but Stricken implied more – that I was exceedingly attractive and never experienced rejection. That was entirely untrue. I tried to understand his frustration and anguish. I was not burdened with ill health and my own mortality as he was. I could not say anything right. He hung up on me.

I stared at the receiver in my shaking hand, then placed it on the table. I could not fault him for what he had done, but I still could not hang it up. Then I laid down flat on my back, my eyes open but unseeing. I willed my tears not to dribble down my cheeks. I tried to steady my breathing.

Weeks later, I tried to call him, but he refused to speak with me. Did he not understand that I did not want to hurt him, but that I did not want to mislead him either? That one could not force things?

Months later, I was home alone when someone messaged that Stricken had passed away. I stared at the words on my screen in disbelief. To find out something of this magnitude in such a casual manner had taken me aback. I had not believed he would die. *Should I have continued seeing him to gladden his last few months on earth?*

I had not personally known anyone as young as Stricken who had died. This time, I could not control the flood of tears. They flowed and flowed. I jumped into the shower trying to wash away my self-loathing, my unforgiven sin, my anger at him, my pain for him, my regrets.

I learned that it is painful to be rejected, but sometimes it's equally painful to turn down someone else. The relentless storm of tears went on and on. I thought of his silver *Kiddush* cup cradled in its velvet box, unused. My tears would have overflowed that cup.

Wishy-Washy-Waity

One day, CoedGuy asked me out. Again, I was not expecting it. I always seemed taken by surprise when asked out. CoedGuy was more modern and had girlfriends. We had many philosophical talks over the months but, at first, I thought he would prefer a woman who shared his background. Over time I saw that though his dress code or past schooling made him appear more modern than me, his Jewish values were very strong. In some ways, they were stronger than mine. He had chosen a date by which he would make *Aliyah* to Israel, whether married or not. So, when he asked me out after months of friendship, I laughed him off. "Of course not," was my first thought, even though I liked him.

As there were so many parallels between CoedGuy and YeshivaGuy, I felt slightly disloyal to the man who had told me to move on. I was loyal to a fault. But I liked CoedGuy, and tried to look past stereotypes, focusing on his character rather than my perception of him, or of what I thought society expected me to marry. This man was not out of bounds, why was I creating boundaries where there needn't be?

I was guilty of judging this book by his cover and realized my mistake. We got along, enjoyed each other's company, spent our free time at *Shabbatonim*, loved the group, and socializing. *Duh!* Why had I been so dense? "I would love to go out," I said. It made sense.

I prepared nervously as though it was a first date with a stranger. I fussed with my hair and makeup. I wore a figure-hugging outfit. I was nervous. What would he think of that awful schoolyard across the street? What would my father say to embarrass me?

But their chit-chat went well, and I could not wait to escape and have our usual one-on-one talks in the car, just the two of us. As I slid my seat belt on, he turned to me and said, "I have never seen you like this before!"

"Well, I gussied up a bit."

"A bit? Are you kidding?" Then enunciating each word, he said, "You. Look. Stunning."

"I, what?" I spotted my father peeking through the venetian blinds. I wanted us to scram out of the driveway.

He laughed, "I know you heard me. I've known you for a long while now, and you have *never* looked like this."

I may have looked better than usual, but I was most definitely not stunning — though I was flattered to hear that word. It would be the only time anyone called me that, which is why I remember it so clearly. True, Stricken had also found me very attractive, but I had dates that would show up and wiggle their noses in displeasure at the sight of me. Beauty is very subjective.

"Can we please go?" My father was still spying on us.

"Yes, madam, whatever you say, madam. Your wish is my command."

We spent a lovely evening having dinner and walking through the brightly lit city streets, talking about everything. I had a glorious time. I felt I could be my true self with him and was sure I would see him again.

But I was wrong.

I didn't even get another phone call. I waited. A week. Another week. A third week. I had known this guy for over a year. We were friends. We had a great time. He had called me "stunning," and now – nothing? None of this made a whit of sense to me. *Could he have been in an accident?*

I asked others if they had seen him. Yes, they said. So, he was not lying broken in some hospital bed. *How dare he? How dare he let me think the worst? How dare he mislead me after a great night like that? How dare he reject me without a word? How dare he treat a friend this way? I would not let him off so easily. No.*

I called him up. There was no Caller ID in those days. We only had human screeners. Someone else would pick up the phone and silently mouth "It's him (or her)" before we'd frantically wave off the call as they made some lame excuse on our behalf for being unable to come to the phone. But CoedGuy had no screener and picked up the phone himself.

"Hi," I said.

"Oooooh, hi!"

"Didn't expect me to call? What is the *matter* with you? You have known me for months now; what on earth has made you change your mind in one evening, probably the best one we spent together? How could you be so.... so wishy-washy, so gutless?"

Nothing.

"Say something!"

"We only went out once," he said.

"I don't care," I said, "we've had many heart-to-heart talks. I deserve better. I deserve an explanation!"

"I'm so sorry. We were talking about *Aliyah* and you seemed sort of open to it, but I'm gung-ho on moving to Israel and I need someone who feels the same," he said.

"You knew all this before you ever asked me out," I countered. I was furious. This was so lame.

"I should've called you...."

"You sure should have."

"... but I didn't want to hurt you."

"That's exactly what you did. You should've discussed it with me. You knew we would run into each other again. What did you think would happen then? Hopefully, someday I can put this behind me."

In time, I did get past it. He eventually married a lovely girl and I danced at their wedding. A few years later, they did make Aliyah.

As for me, I went back to crossing off days on my little calendar, wishing and waiting for YeshivaGuy to come back from Israel. Nothing else was working.

Disconnected

I was not connecting to the men I met on setups. When I thought about the men I was pining over, I realized that with each one I had developed an emotional intimacy prior to dating. The stress of blind dating did not exist when I met someone as a pen-pal or at a *Shabbaton*. There was no need to decide right away. It was easier to develop a pressure-free bond. The structure of blind dating felt unnatural to me.

If I was not sure about someone at a party or while messaging, I could give it time or see him at the next *Shabbaton*. When a blind date asked me for a second date, if I wasn't certain whether I was interested or not, the decision carried so much more weight. If I said "yes," he could misconstrue it as interest rather than a

"I-don't-know-so-I-want-to-give-it-another-shot." I would feel guilty to have the guy treat me to dinner on wrong assumptions. On the other hand, if I said "no," would I be throwing away a good opportunity? Would yet another matchmaker berate me for my choices?

I didn't know how to handle these doubts. I was allowing them to affect me much more than they should have, and it was draining me emotionally. It is hard to please matchmakers, one's date, and oneself, all at the same time. Mostly, I felt I was trying too hard to please everyone else, but I wasn't feeling good about any of it for myself. Dating had not turned out to be as I had imagined it would be.

I met guys at *Shabbatonim* and in college, but none of them felt right.

One student talked angrily about the world and told me he punched holes in walls. He created a mixtape for me and I loved the music, but I envisioned myself a battered wife if I married him. He had anger issues. Scratch that one.

Another guy's sentences were limited to two or three words. He liked listening to me, which is probably why I enjoyed talking to him at first, but he had nothing to say for himself. I felt somebody ought to shake a bit of chocolate and strawberry into him because he was way too vanilla.

Then there was a bearded, heavyset guy who was very bright and well-mannered. On our third date he had a strange look on his face and asked me if I was playing a practical joke on him. Was I me or my sister? Had we switched places? I was not wearing the same make-up as the last time, and apparently, I looked like a completely different person to him. We had a good laugh about that. He was someone I should've given more of a chance. I was not immediately comfortable with him, but he was a good person and very well-spoken to boot. I should've tried harder.

Looking back, he was one of several mistakes I made in my early dating years. Perhaps every time a young man was a real possibility, my fear sabotaged any chance I had. Every little uncertainty or doubt was magnified beyond reason instead of being worked through.

Me

What was wrong with me? Was I sabotaging myself? Doing my *hishtadlus?* Putting in real effort to meet my mate? Was I subconsciously afraid of marriage? Did I fear hurting my older sister? Was I not ready? Would I ever be? Would I ever marry?

I thought of everything I had done to get a step closer – applications, fees, *Shabbatonim, shadchanim;* parties, lectures; meeting this one, that one, and the other one who may know someone; going to many kind strangers' homes for Shabbos meals or weekends because there *may* be someone to meet; hours-long bus rides to events, missed buses, schlepping luggage on buses and trains; traveling out of town to meet new faces; getting *brachos* from holy people; *davening* for myself as well as praying for others; *Shir Hashirim, Tehillim,* my own prayers, and every conceivable *segulah,* including midnight prayers, fasting; giving *tzedakah* to poor brides; graciously setting up my friends with men who had rejected me; going online before most anyone else; opening myself up to men who were far more or far less religious than I was to find a possible bridge to our common humanity; discovering human nature in all its many, many shades; and mostly, learning the lesson of humility.

I thought of all the audacious questions I had been asked that ripped away any shred of privacy, and the people who asked them – the matchmakers, acquaintances, strangers, doctors, dates. How old are you exactly? What does your father do? How old are you? Are you *shomer negiah?* How old are you? Why aren't you married? How old are you? Are you gay? How old are you? Do you know what you're missing? How old are you? Are you a virgin? How old are you? What's wrong with you? Why don't you like him? How old are you? Are you *sure* you want to get married? How old are you? Are you engaged? You look engaged with that new haircut! You know that, right? Are you fertile? Do you realize I can't set you up if I don't know that? The questions would echo on.

One of the most irritating questions for me was "Have you gone on vacation?" I could not abide a certain tone, or the filling-in-the-gap-of-silence when one awkwardly grasps for something – anything – to say to a single person. People fall back on the vacation question as though no other aspect of life concerned singles. Did people realize that singles don't necessarily have a built-in partner to go on vacation or spend holidays with – that we often have to scramble to make plans or go solo? Every time I heard that question asked in that tone of voice, I cringed. Does this person think that all singles do is party and vacation? True, we usually have more free time and less obligations, but we also have parents to care for, jobs to support ourselves, health to worry about, and we too can't escape the mundane chores of everyday life.

I told myself they didn't know what to say, but I couldn't help the way this question grated on my nerves more than it should have. It made me feel like I'd become a "cautionary tale" -- *don't end up like her or you won't have anything in your life but "vacation."*

When my nieces and nephews entered the picture, inevitably at some point it would dawn on them, one by one, that I lived alone. Every couple of years, I recognized the mental calculation followed by the troubled expression on their adorable round faces. And they'd ask, "How come there is no Tatty? Couldn't you find one? How does everyone else find one? Do you say *Kiddush* and *Havdalah* yourself?"

I wished I could erase their fears and reassure them that my fate would not be theirs. My heart would crack with love when some of them, at tender ages, approached men in *shul* and said, "I have a very nice *tante*. Would you like to marry her?"

I reflected on all the conflicting advice I was given by anyone who crossed my path. Dress up nice. Dress casual. Lie about your age. Don't lie about your age. Don't worry, it will happen at the right time. If you sit back and relax, nothing will happen. Rejection makes you stronger. It's a learning experience. Put your best face forward. Be yourself. Give him a chance. Give him another chance. You don't need to have anything in common. So what if you have nothing to talk about? Hold your nose and jump in. Find a therapist. Speak to a rabbi. Do *mitzvos*. Try this *segulah*. Try that one. Focus on marriage. Really. Just. Focus.

36

I thought of "women" who were afflicted with amnesia the day they married and were suddenly full of practical advice that they themselves had never heeded as "girls." Or those who had completely forgotten me altogether in their busy, new lives.

There were others who relished reminding me that I was no longer young, or that their time was precious as though mine was less so, or that *they* were doing *me* the *chesed* (even when I'd never asked them for help). *Chesed* is most often translated as "an act of loving kindness." In *Leviticus* 20:17 the word is defined by its lesser known definition as "disgrace" or "abomination." When one fails to consider the feelings or wishes of a recipient, a *chesed* intended as a good deed can quickly shift into disgrace.

I recalled a zealous woman who'd told me she had become religious and had prayed mightily for six months straight. God had subsequently found her a husband. If only I'd do the same, God would help me too. Or the man who had been a serial dater, finally gotten serious and married, advised me to consider dating a *baal teshuvah* because as soon as he did, he got engaged. I had been doing all that from the start, before they'd had their miraculous lightbulb moments. I didn't bother telling them what I really thought of their advice or how their words made me feel.

All this unsolicited counsel buffeted and shaped me in ways I did not imagine. I was on a soul-crushing emotional merry-go-round of: Hope. Desire. Rage. Rejection. Pain. Humility. Confidence. Injustice. Jealousy. Optimism. Faith. Pessimism. Indignity. Longing. Despair. Love. Sacrifice. Acceptance.

Then I came to realize – it's not about me, after all. It's about You, God. You.

PART TWO

Like a Rose Among Thorns (Song of Songs 2:2)

כשושנה בין החוחים (שיר השירים ב:ב)

Coed Chaos

A whiskered Philippine guy in the computer lab followed me around like a puppy and asked me out again and again. I'd tell Whiskers over and over that I wanted someone with my Jewish values.

He said I was a racist, but smiled. I figured he was trying to use any and all ammunition at his disposal. He didn't appear angry, but I felt I should explain. I told him that if he were a Jewish Philippine, he might be a contender, but this was about religious values and lifestyle, not race. No matter what I said, he didn't understand me. Maybe it was the language barrier. I don't know how long he'd been in the US and his English was good, but not perfect.

I could not avoid him. He worked in the computer lab where we all went to print and process our programs. Computer science classes finished later than others and then we had to go to the computer lab as well, so by the time I walked to the bus stop no one else was there. Whiskers decided it was not safe for me to stand at the bus stop by myself at 10:00 pm, so he showed up. I didn't want to be at the bus stop alone with him, so I told him that if anyone religious saw me with him, it would ruin my entire reputation. Of course, it was not true, but he didn't have to know that. So, he left. Then one night, I saw him there again. He was standing five or six feet away.

I marched over, "Hi Whiskers, waiting for the bus?"

"Nah, I have a car."

"Then what are you standing here for?"

"What you think? You think I can do my job inside when I know you're standing alone outside at this hour? I'm good man. I do not ruin your religion reputation."

I walked back to my spot and he stayed in his. It was weird. It was dark. It was uncomfortable. For the next few weeks, he was always at the bus stop. Sometimes there were one or two other people and sometimes not, but he always stood a few feet away.

One winter night, I had just missed the bus and it was snowing. I was in for a long wait and I knew it. It was freezing and desolate out there, and I didn't think Whiskers would show up. But after twenty minutes or so, when my toes were numb, he did. I was secretly happy. There were no buses in sight. He yelled out, "Can I step closer, religious lady?"

"Yes..."

"Listen, you will freeze. I have car. I can take you home."

"Oh, no. No way. My father will see us, and how will I explain?"

"Just listen, lady. I will drop you off at your corner. See? No bad reputation."

He was wearing me down. I squinted into the distance. There were no headlights anywhere in sight. I was frozen. I could not feel my fingers or toes. I relented.

We sat in the car together and I could sense his unspoken victory. He was happy. He reminded me of the turtle taking baby step after baby step to reach his goal. But he hadn't reached his goal because I would never agree to go out with him. He dropped me off at the corner as promised. He waited till he saw me turn into the house. Then he zoomed by as I watched through the little glass panel in the door. Nothing had happened, but I felt guilty. He was going to expect a payoff he would never get. Was I using him? I was not encouraging this in any way. I would not do it again. But after the next class, it was raining and freezing. There were other people standing at the stop with me, but he stood there in the rain waiting anyhow.

This time he said, "You silly lady, it's wet and cold." I weighed my options. I would not be waiting alone. There were two others, but it was frigid and he had delivered me safely last time. We went to get his car and he started the engine to warm the car. I was bundled up in my down coat, and thank God for that – because the next thing I knew, he had made a pass at me. *God!*

I recoiled in shock. I could smell his spicy breath. I could feel those whiskers brush my skin. *Ew! This was totally my fault.*

His weight against me felt heavy with his thick coat. Thank God for the coats. I blamed myself. I *knew* he was going to expect a payoff. How foolish could I be? He had never tried to get to know me. All he had done was pester me to go out with him, compliment me, and strategize to get me alone. I was too smart and too religious to get into this dumb situation.

"Back off!"

Whiskers laughed, thinking I was playing hard-to-get. Then he saw the look on my face and retreated, protesting, "This is high school stuff!" *Not for me. Not my high school.* That I was sure of.

I opened the car door. "I'll drive you home," he said contritely, "and I promise I won't come near you." I was more angry than afraid. The rain was coming down in sheets. It was freezing outside and he had always kept his word. I shut the door and we rode in silence. I was angrier at myself than him. I had learned that the rabbis understood human nature exceedingly well. He didn't live by my guidelines. I shouldn't have expected him to. *Why had I been so naive?*

He did keep his word, as always, and did not touch me again. He dropped me off at the corner. I walked home without looking back or opening an umbrella. I wanted the rain to wash this whole episode away.

But it did not. It stayed with me for months and filled me with guilt. *What would YeshivaGuy think? Was I still worthy of him?* I felt tainted. Nothing much had happened. But the memory of Whisker's hot breath and his wiry whiskers made me cringe. I recalled the verse in seventh grade. *Was I too sure of myself?* God knew the truth, but if people knew, would they forgive me? I was hard on myself. I wanted YeshivaGuy to be back. The year was over, he should be back by now.

I spoke to God. *If I want to meet and marry a nice Jewish man with my values, why are You throwing Whiskers in my path instead? Help me to do Your will.*

The summer was nearly over and I was going to a barbecue in YeshivaGuy's neighborhood. My heart ached for YeshivaGuy and as I walked from the subway to the barbecue, I could not help but think about him and wonder whether he was back and when he would call. I prayed, "God, is he back? Is he the one I'm supposed to marry?" I waited to cross the street and a car backed out of a corner parking spot and pulled away. The newly exposed license plate of the car parked ahead of it, read "YeshivaGuy" *Oh. My. God.* It could not possibly be his car. For one thing, he hadn't had one before he left, and he surely wouldn't have had time to get a car with a vanity plate in so short a time even if he had already returned.

Wow. I definitely felt it was a sign directly from God telling me he was back. At the barbecue, someone confirmed that they had seen him that week. I was elated. I could finally, finally go out with him.

But he didn't call.

I hated myself for calling him. It didn't bode well, but we had promised each other to meet, no matter what. He was the man I wanted to marry, so I swallowed my pride and called.

He didn't sound thrilled to hear from me. He said he had changed throughout the year and wanted someone more religious. He had "*frummed* out." I guiltily thought of Whiskers. Of course, God was punishing me. This was not a coincidence at all.

He then went on to say that it would be a complete waste of time – *bitul zman* – to go out with me or talk to me, as he was sure he would not marry me. I hadn't waited an entire year to discover I was nothing to him but a waste of time. I lashed out, "No, this is most definitely not acceptable, mister. If you're more religious now, then you better make sure you keep your word. You said we would meet again, no matter what! I'm sorry if you lost interest, but I need closure. I spent a year staring at the calendar. I'm not asking you. I'm telling you to keep your word." He reluctantly agreed. My sister thought I'd be punishing myself. But I had spent a year doing it his way. I needed to see this through for myself my way.

He came to pick me up and opened the door for me. Then, to my astonishment, he said, "Wait, this is not a real date, is it? It's closure!" He slammed the car door shut before I went in. Did a year in yeshiva turn a nice young man into a learned scholar at the cost of basic manners? I was horrified, and blinked back the tears. I would not open this door on my own after that slam. I prayed my father wasn't peeking out the window this time. I stood stubbornly waiting for him to come back and open the door, which he finally did.

He asked whether I had met other men. Well, I had, but nothing I wanted to talk about. "Did you meet anyone?" I asked, afraid of the answer.

"Actually, I met someone on the plane. We dated a few months." *On the plane? Before he even entered Israeli airspace? Before I had even crossed ONE day off the strip calendar? They had dated a few months?*

I was gutted. Surely this was a punishment! Any shred of hope was gone. I had also lost any desire to give another yeshiva guy the chance to mess with my heart. I had felt unworthy of him because of Whiskers — but really, who was unworthy of whom here?

Workload

The next few months I plodded along, carrying the weight of my heavy heart. I was busy with work and school and just shut out dating. I had to nurse my heart back to health. I no longer trusted my instincts.

I worked on the tenth floor of a small midtown building and when the elevator stopped on the ninth floor, which was an audio studio, there was a receptionist at the front desk with her long, long, cornrows. She would look up, break into a smile and wave. I waved back. It took months until I finally got off the elevator and introduced myself to her. She told me they produced audio for commercials.

Then one day, on the elevator, one of the technicians that often got off on that floor, turned around and flashed a set of beautiful teeth that look so white against his dark skin. "I've seen you before, and you always wave to CornRow. I'm Jr.Engineer."

"She always waves to me too," I said. I introduced myself and he got off on 9, turned around and I waved to both of them.

In the following weeks, I'd see him in the elevator and he always seemed genuinely happy to cross paths with me. I was curious about his work. He saw that I was a religious Jew and asked about that.

"Are you like the guys in the Diamond District?" he asked. I'd often peer through the glittering windows just a few blocks away, picking out my fantasy engagement ring. The streets swarmed with Chassidim and Litvaks scurrying around in dark suits, beards, hats.

"I suppose, but we're all different levels of observance. May I ask what nationality you are?"

"Guess," he said.

"Hmm… that is tough to guess. Are you a mix of two races?" I was afraid to guess wrong and insult him.

"Which two?"

"Umm… are you from South America?"

"No, I was born in the Bronx," he said in perfect English. He had no accent, but he had exotic eyes, curly hair and thick lips.

"Are you half black?"

"No."

"I give up."

He laughed, "I'm American, of Puerto Rican heritage."

"Puerto Rican?"

"You're that surprised?"

"Well, yeah. You just shattered my stereotype of Puerto Ricans."

"I did? Guess that's good. The women I meet just want one thing. But I noticed your modesty and am drawn to that. I feel comfortable with you. I can be myself. I don't have to put on an act."

44

Here we go again, God. Here is another guy I will have to walk away from. Why do you send decent, nice gentiles my way? Is this a test? My Jewish dates don't know how or what to talk about. When I'm not interested in them, they don't get the hint. When I am interested, they dump me. My heart is shredded.

I was talking to God more and more aside from my ritual prayers. Would I tire God out with my non-stop chatter?

Jr.Engineer was a balm to my shredded heart and self-esteem. He let me know that I was likable and worthy. He told me I had substance, while matchmakers were telling me I was not giving men a chance, that I was picky, I was no spring chicken, I was not really serious about marriage. I knew that not to be the case. I just needed to feel the same ease of conversation that I had with Jr.Engineer with a Jewish guy. I prayed to God to send that man to me.

I had one more night semester left and then I wanted to quit my job to go to Israel. What would be the harm in talking to a good soul for a short while? Would it hurt me? Would it heal me? I didn't know what to do.

One day I came to work feeling ill, but my boss and co-workers were all out. I wanted to lock up and leave, but couldn't leave the office unattended without telling my boss. I dialed him at home, but there was no answer. I laid down on the carpet curling into a fetal position, feeling nauseous, and not knowing what to do. The phone rang, but I could not jump up quickly enough to answer it. *This is bad.*

Finally, I stumbled to the elevator clutching my belly, and made my way down to CornRow and told her how ill I felt. She called Jr.Engineer from the back to get me ginger ale, but when he came out front, I had to run to their restroom. It turned out to be food poisoning from the takeout I had eaten the previous night. CornRow and Jr.Engineer took care of me till I stopped trembling and Jr.Engineer joked "One look at me, and you vomit, huh?" I joked back, "One look at you, and I'm cured." But I was not cured at all. I was heartsick and confused.

Over the next few weeks, I had a few more blind dates.

"How many sisters and brothers do you have?" while slurping spaghetti.

45

"*What does your father do for a living?*" as I watched him scratch dandruff into his soup.

"*Wow, you're ugly,*" said another with a triple chin.

I did not want my beauty or lack of it rated to my face. I did not want them all asking the same questions, as though it were off a prepared questionnaire. They were grilling me as if I were interviewing for a job called "Wife." When I refused a second date with these men, the matchmakers would get cross with me. The tension of all my heartache that I was trying to bury – enduring dreadful dates while distancing myself from unsuitable company I was drawn to – was building up.

I wanted real conversation. I had those on my lunch breaks at work with Jr.Engineer. We talked about music, art, science and history. I was never bored, but always worried. One day he told me his brother was taking him on a weeklong skiing trip to Hunter Mountain, and I was amazed because I was going the week after his trip for an overnight with my sister to the very same place. Neither of us had ever skied before, but our siblings had. Both of us were terrified and excited that we would be learning a week apart. We decided he'd hide a message somewhere and then give me clues to find them. We weren't going together, which set me at ease, but I felt as excited as though we were.

This was a special trip for my sister and me. We rarely did things like this. She was a very good skier and I had never gone. We decided to go during the week, away from the weekend crowds. The snow was soft, glistening in the sunlight and the slopes were empty. It was serene. I was terrified of skiing, but I kept thinking that Jr.Engineer had been on this mountain just the week before. It gave me some courage. I had taken a beginner lesson, but I had no experience. My sister and I rode up the lift on the smallest mountain, and she offered to help. I whizzed down and the speed frightened me because I had no control whatsoever. Nothing I had learned in the lesson worked to slow me down. I was afraid of crashing into a tree at this speed, so I bent my knees, stretched my arms out and made myself fall to the side. I was bruised and cold, but I had momentarily felt the thrill of the speed. It was enough. My sister wanted to ski some more, so I brushed the snow off myself and headed to the lodge to search for Jr.Engineer's note. He had given me some clues. I searched till I found his note stuck between a locker and the wall behind it. It said "Had a blast. Hope you do too. With love, Jr.Engineer."

"*With love.*" *Sigh.*

My heart warmed, but I could not explain anything to anyone. I could not explain to him why a relationship was impossible. I could not explain to matchmakers what was wrong with my Jewish dates. I could not explain to myself why this note hidden a week earlier affected me so strongly. He had been here, but we weren't even together. This was all upside down. I was speeding down the mountain and I feared I was going to crash.

When I returned to work, I was eager to tell Jr.Engineer I had found his note, and he was excited to tell me that he had fallen in love with skiing. He had mastered it over his week and would now go weekly with his brother. Then he told me more about his brother. He was divorced and had been married to a Jewish woman. They didn't get divorced because of her Judaism, but had gotten married in spite of it. Why was my religion a problem? He didn't understand. It was racist. There it was again. The same question and accusation.

I turned it on God. *I am a religious woman trying to meet a religious man and I need Your help. Please explain it to me. Why do I have rapport with the men who are all wrong for me?* In early twentieth century Poland and Lithuania, men attended yeshiva and women had no Jewish education, so there was a religious gap between them. Many of the women assimilated and intermarried, but here I was with a strong Jewish education with the will and desire to marry someone who shared my Jewish values.

Help me! Tell me, God, why is this happening? I am going to quit my job when I graduate college, and I am going to Israel for the whole summer. I want to get closer to You and I want to meet someone I can marry. Will You help me?

I would not stay in touch with Jr.Engineer for much longer. He told me his company was moving a month before I planned on quitting.

Thank You God. Are You making this easier for me? But I was in pain. I had grown fond of him, as much as I tried to keep him at arm's length. He gave me what I didn't get elsewhere. It would be hard to let him go. But the timing was right.

He was mad that I let my beliefs come between us, but that's because they were my beliefs, not his. I was mad at my fate and wanted things to be different. I wanted things to work out for me. We made up to go out one time. We had never done so, but we would – to say goodbye.

On that last day, we left our office building together and went all the way downtown to Battery Park to watch the sun set. We had no words. The stars appeared and we sat in silence. He took my hand in his. *God forgive me, but I liked it.* He had never touched me before and I knew I shouldn't let him now either; but we were not starting anything, we were ending it. He played with my fingers tentatively, testing me. I didn't react, so he sandwiched my hand in his. My eyes misted. The stars multiplied in my tears.

That night, he was supposed to meet his brother to go on their weekly skiing weekend so he had to find a public phone. We found one on the street and he dialed, no answer. We walked some more. I was in a dream state, sleepwalking along. It was dark and we didn't see any public phones, so we went into a building to search for one. There were some beautiful wooden phone booths in the lobby, the kind with folding doors that Clark Kent would emerge from, changed into his Superman persona. He went in and dialed and reached his brother. His brother was finishing up work and he would have to start heading uptown to meet him soon.

He hung up. I was standing in the doorway. So, this was it.

I knew it was right to end things, but I didn't want it to end. We stood inches apart and I gazed into his liquid brown eyes, trying to imprint the memory. I thought of all the people who would cluck in disapproval at this friendship, as well as all the people who would scoff and say it was really nothing. But people were not my main concern, God was. What I wanted very much to know was would God know how hard I was struggling to do the right thing? Would God measure the pain branded in me by other men? The trials I had endured? What my inner thoughts and feelings were and that this was my goodbye? Could an Almighty God know what it's like to not be Almighty? To be powerless and human? Most of all, how would God judge me?

Jr.Engineer wiped my tears away and reached for my hand again. I let him. We walked away from the phone booth, and like Superman, I was changed. We crossed the lobby and exited the building. Our breaths floated between us in wispy clouds. Then we let our hands slide apart and without another word, walked in opposite directions. I never saw or spoke to him again.

A Real Crash

I had notified my boss at the design firm that I would be quitting when I graduated. I wanted to go to Israel for the summer. We did beautiful design work in that place, and I was not sure what kind of job I'd get when I returned. Maybe I would try to switch over to computer science, as that was my major. I was afraid that I'd be stuck with nothing. I lacked confidence. I was young, but felt old and washed up. I needed to get away.

I had never had a gap year. I had gone to college at night for over five years while working during the day. I still lived at home and was single, so I had relative financial freedom.

I was scared to quit, but I did it. I gave my boss five-weeks' notice as a courtesy, because I didn't want to leave him stranded. I was finishing up school and would stay till graduation.

But before my time was up, I received an unexpected call at the office on a Friday afternoon. My cousin, who was an EMT, cryptically told me that my father had called him. "Your mother is ok, but she's been taken to Bellevue Hospital."

"Bellevue? Isn't that where the crazy people go? How could she be ok if she's there?"

My mother had been hit by a truck in downtown Brooklyn and was seriously injured. I had been fearful of "crashing," prayed not to "crash;" and here, instead of my metaphorical crash was the real thing, and my mother was the victim. She had been taken to Bellevue because they specialized in microsurgery. I had a short window of time to run over there, check on her, and then get home to prepare for Shabbos. My father and brother would stay in the *Bikur Cholim* apartment near the hospital.

My mother required multiple surgeries. We had no idea if she would ever walk again. I was going to cancel my trip, but my mother did not want me to. So, I waited to see what would happen. If the surgeries were successful, she'd need months of therapy. My boss had already found a replacement and refused to give my job back. Life was not fair. Losing a job unfairly was bad, but my mother had lost so much more. Others in the ICU had lost their mobility, limbs, or fingers. That put things into perspective quickly. Did I cause this, I wondered? My guilt over Jr.Engineer still weighed heavily on me.

Being unemployed gave me time to spend with my mother and to care for her. When she finally came home, she needed assistance. It took weeks till she was ready for physical therapy. I was able to drive her to appointments and keep her company. Then she pushed me to go to Israel, as I had already lost my job for it. I rescheduled a new and shorter trip. It would be hard to leave her, and harder still to have what I hoped would be the best summer of my life while she was having her worst.

The Holy Land

A few months later, I went to Israel and wanted to do what I could to meet other young people. I joined a singles' Israel tour, but did not find out till the last moment that the tour would be all male – ten of them, a *minyan* – except for me and one other female. The odds were great I would meet someone. Luckily OneOtherFemale and I got along well because when I met the Minyan, my heart sank.

The only man on that tour I enjoyed conversing with was the tour leader, and he was engaged. One of the Minyan guys was decent, but

50

our personalities and observance level did not mesh, and he had a bad stutter. He had trouble talking, but at least he had what to say when he did. But, my God, the other men were all socially inept. I had already met awkward men on blind dates, but that was one man at a time. Here was an entire group that had trouble communicating. They all seemed to have jobs that require advanced degrees. They were clearly book smart, but not street smart. I tried to carry the conversations, but I was doing all the lifting. And with the added load of my own heavy heart, I just found the weight overbearing. *I can't do this.* I would just have to find my own way to have fun with the tour guide and OneOtherFemale.

One evening we were in the port of Haifa strolling along the twinkling, lighted boardwalk when we ran into American Marines walking towards us. Our group stopped to talk to them and next to these buffed, toned men, with closely cropped haircuts wearing neatly pressed and sharply pleated uniforms, the guys we were with, seemed disheveled and out of shape. There were IDF guys around the port too, but these Americans had stopped to greet their fellow Americans and were hard to miss – they were bigger, taller, more muscular. Even the shortest one, who was a black man, seemed so fit and muscular that he, too, appeared to tower over the taller men in our group who hunched over and seemed uncomfortable in their own skin. It was his confidence more than his height, that gave him that appearance.

They told us they had read about Jews in the Bible, but until their ship had pulled into the Haifa port, they had never met any. The short black Marine and his tall friend who had almond-shaped eyes were talking to OneOtherFemale and me. They were from Georgia and Oklahoma. I was irritated by the men on the tour, as well as the tough-talking assertive Israelis we encountered. These young men were sweet and refined, saying "Yes, ma'am," and politely asking us questions about "the Jews." They were heart-poundingly handsome – anyone could see that – but I had quit my job and traveled to Israel with hopes of meeting my Jewish soulmate. I didn't need or want a heart-pounder, though the flirting had re-sparked my female instincts that had been reduced to dying embers on this tour.

51

Some of the Minyan men were conversing with the Marines as well, but mostly they were just hanging back silently, watching "their" girls animatedly talking up the Marines. They probably were wondering how they could not manage to do whatever it was the Marines were doing. The black man asked if I'd like to be his pen-pal. I really didn't want to, because where could it lead? However, I didn't want him to think a white girl was saying no to a black man. I gave him my address. The tall almond-eyed one asked if he could also have it, so how could I say no? When we parted, OneOtherFemale said, "What did you do that for? They're not Jewish!"

"I know, but you were flirting with them too!"

"You're crazy."

"No, what's crazy is that I came to meet Jewish guys and we're on a tour with ten men, TEN! Yet, we cannot have any substantive conversation with any of them. That's what's crazy. Don't you agree? I couldn't say no to the black guy."

"Why not?"

"Because non-Jewish guys always think I'm racist when I say no. This one would for sure! I didn't want to hurt his feelings."

"Well, our guys' feelings got hurt," she said.

"Why? I've been trying to engage with them at every meal, every outing. I do try. They're the ones not trying!" I protested. "Anyhow these Marines won't write. They meet and flirt with women in every port. I promise, in a few minutes, they'll forget all about us."

A few weeks after my return home, I would find out I was wrong once again.

The tour was over, and I had signed up with a young adult group to volunteer at a *moshav*. However, with my luck – or by God's design – once again, this failed. I was the sole participant to sign up and was not told in advance. I arrived at the *moshav* and lived with a family whose home was filthy. I tried to feed the baby, but his face was a fly trap. I kept waving them off but dozens of flies were feeding off the baby food crusted around his lips. I had nothing to wipe his mouth with. It was disgusting – the heat, the flies, the dirt. His diaper had not been changed, I couldn't find any others, and he stunk. The mother handed me a soggy paper plate of spaghetti for my dinner – no proteins, no vegetables. I understood they were poor, and I wasn't expecting much, but I had no appetite for wet spaghetti and flies floating in watery ketchup. The house smelled sour. I felt faint and too listless to eat.

There were no singles here. No group activities. *What was I doing here?* I had expected other volunteers and a campfire *kumzitz*, perhaps a way to meet Jewish men. I knew the going would be tough, and I would gladly tough it out, if I had one friend in that place – even female. But I did not.

The next day a large cardboard box of used clothing arrived from the US at the *moshav*. The women there asked me to help them sort the garments. As they picked through the clothing, they discarded half the items, complaining about the size, the color, how worn-out they were, and mocked the Americans who had sent them "*shmattehs.*" Sitting there silently, I thought, "Beggars can't be choosers." I had not complained about my stringy-fly-ketchup dinner. I had merely put it aside. I couldn't listen to this ingratitude – it angered me. The American community had collected and shipped these boxes in goodwill and now these women were disparaging their efforts.

I told one of the ladies that I was applying for graduate school. She brushed off the remark, said I should focus on marriage, and forget about career. I *was* much more focused on marriage and I *was* burnt out after five years of night school. But considering their poverty, I didn't think furthering my education, especially as I was still single, was such a terrible idea.

Even our holy ancestors and sages had jobs. Moses was a shepherd. Rambam was Sultan Saladin's physician. Many of our leaders had jobs along with their faith in God. Our sages didn't rely on government subsidies, and certainly were not sorting through used clothing and complaining to boot.

I had to get away from this lethargic outpost in the desert. Besides, Shiva Asar b'Tammuz, a major fast day, was arriving. I needed a nutritious meal before a long fast like that.

I left before my week was up and went to visit my uncle and aunt. My aunt asked me why I wasn't married yet. It was always her first question. I was way past nineteen, and as my young cousins were married off, she determined to find me a husband too. I didn't have confidence in her ability. Could she understand my American sensibilities, my observance level? She had barely seen me over the years. Did she understand my personality and needs? Who would she find for me? She was a tough Israeli, who drove an ambulance for the IDF, as well as tour buses, when not mothering. We spoke in a smattering mixture of Hebrew and Yiddish, with some English and French thrown in. We barely communicated, so how would she find me a man?

She came up with a "perfect match" for me.

"Really?"

"Yes, yes he has the same last name as you!"

I groaned, guessing this would probably be the only thing we had in common. We lived in two different countries, and he was a blue-collar bus driver like her, while I was a college-educated professional. As I did not have the backbone to argue with her, I relented. Then she told me, it would be a great idea if I accompanied him on one of his group tours on the upcoming fast day. *How do I get myself into these circumstances?*

I boarded the bus with him and a busload of senior citizens. He was only fluent in Hebrew, and with an entire bus as our audience, the awkwardness multiplied. I sat up front near the tour guide, but I didn't talk to the driver. The bus was crowded with chattering passengers. The vinyl seat was already sticking to me. I was sweating and needed water, but it was a fast day.

How was this a date? Had my aunt twisted his arm as well? Was he also seething at her? That would be another thing we had in common aside from our last name. After his *Shalom, how are you?* He made no effort to make me comfortable or speak to me. *This was a looney idea.* I was mad at my aunt and even madder at myself. I was sitting there fuming. This was already a day of mourning; I didn't need a new reason to mourn. I had stewed long enough. I did not know how far he would travel, but I had no intention of spending the entire day, perspiring and thirsting on a bus with strangers who would merrily snack, drink and laugh, oblivious to the Jewish fast day, while on their trip. This was no date. We hadn't left Jerusalem yet, but I made up my mind – I was done. "Stop! I'm not well. I need to get off." I felt like a liar, even though it was true. I did not feel well at all. He pulled over and didn't protest or ask me if he could do anything for me. He simply stopped the bus and let me off. I was relieved and disgraced all at once.

How could this happen to me? I walked till I found a little park where I could collect myself. I sat there and took out my *Tehillim*. I felt better sitting under a tree in the park, saying psalms. My eyes were stinging from that humiliation. I would spend time sitting here, imploring God.

It was a while before I felt eyes on me. There was an Israeli man sitting across the park, looking at me. When I looked up, he waved and smiled. I waved back. He sauntered over and I welcomed speaking with him, as I was not eager to return to my aunt any time soon nor walk around in the stifling heat on a fast day.

I asked him why he was hanging out in a park in the middle of a heatwave, and he told me his story. He had been a soldier in the Lebanon War in 1982. A bomb had shattered his shoulder and right arm and blown his thumb off.

"See?" he stretched his palm out. Six years later, he still needed physical therapy for his arm.

"My wife was seven months pregnant and on her way to the hospital to visit me, when she was killed in a car crash." His eyes were red. "That's why I'm thirty-six, with gray hair." He told me he'd been religious till his father fell off the fourth floor of a construction site, landed on and was impaled by a branch of a tree and killed. His stories were so tragic as well as fantastical, I didn't know whether I should believe him. But his eyes moistened at the memories. I didn't think one could fake that.

He told me he was sitting and thinking about Lebanon. "Beirut was a beautiful city and the women were even more beautiful." I interrupted in defense to say Israel had its share of beauties. But he shook his head "No, no. I was thinking of the beautiful women in Beirut, and then I saw you like a mirage across the park and I couldn't believe it. You are so beautiful and *adine*... ah..."

Give me a break. He was sounding like the typical smooth Israeli flirt and my faith in him crumbled fast. He was surely trying to manipulate this naive American. I would've left at this point, but I had a long afternoon ahead of me and nowhere to go. Even though I was no longer sure I could believe him, I felt recovered from that awful bus "date." His stories *were* entertaining, whether or not they were true. I told him about my mother's accident, however his gruesome stories topped mine. He had family and friends who lost everything from their eyeballs, arms, legs, to their life. I could not tell whether he was being truthful or lying just to garner my sympathy.

"You are the woman I have been waiting for my entire life!" *Yeah, right, Prince Charming. Maybe you want a green card?* I hated that crazy-intense Israeli mentality, so I turned the conversation to the fast, the destruction of the Temple, our Jewish education, and backgrounds. He wanted to stay in touch, but I said no. He was not religious, was much older than me, and we lived in different countries. Really, what was the point?

I didn't care for the guy's aggressive style, but I thought it was touching how two strangers could randomly cross paths and offer each other what they both needed at the time – a momentary one-on-one connection – however fleeting. There are people in our lives that we never connect with, so to have this afternoon with him transformed my fast day from an unbearable humiliation to tolerable sorrow.

Later, when I returned to my aunt's house, she said "It must've been a great date, you were out all day." I said it was. I was too angry with her to tell her the truth. I knew by the time she saw and spoke to the bus driver I'd be long gone.

Dodging Darts

I returned to New York, and my luck did not get any better. One "boy" I was set up with, took me to Central Park. We found an ice cream cart and he promptly announced that we were going Dutch. I ended up buying my own ice cream cone, but he had left a bad taste in my mouth for two dollars.

There was a lecherous guy who couldn't keep his eyeballs at our table. They followed each attractive woman as she passed our table. He swiveled his head back over his shoulders. He wanted another date, but I was not interested in watching him watch other women again.

There was the short guy with the Napoleon complex. As we were about to cross a street, he stepped off the curb before me, which made him a few inches shorter. He made a show of jumping back up onto the curb. I pretended I hadn't noticed. But he had noticed that I had noticed, and he declared it was not safe to stand in the gutter. He was not ashamed of his height. No, no, no. He was proud. I said there was nothing wrong with being short. But I felt like an amazon next to him and was not attracted to his defensive manner. When he called me for another date, I turned him down. He sputtered, "I just wanted to see what you would say, but I am not at all interested in asking you out again. So, we're lucky we're on the same page about that."

"We sure are," I said.

There was the sweaty guy who nervously studied his plate. I watched each spaghetti slurp its way up and into his mouth. He did not try to engage in any conversation. I lost my appetite and decided to study my plate as well, as I could not bear to look at him any longer. I did not understand how he thought he could marry anyone if he made no effort whatsoever.

I was baffled that anyone could think these men would be matches for me. Were they playing darts and hoping something would hit a target? I did not want to be any matchmaker's guinea pig or dartboard.

Then there was Cool&Kind. He did not seem my type at all, but I was not sure what my type was anymore. He knew how to talk to women. His hair was a little longish. His smile a little lopsided. His hands were always scrunched into the pockets of his beat-up leather jacket. He was short, but he had soft brown eyes and a dimple. He had a I'm-too-cool-to-be-nice aura about him, even though he was nice.

57

When he asked a mutual friend to find out if I would date him, I was surprised but thrilled to be sought out by him. I had seen him around at parties and never thought we were a match. I was trying to not allow my expectations to play any part here. I wanted to go in with an open mind. We had a nice dinner and pleasant conversation.

I was willing to give it another shot, if he would. He called me, but I was very surprised by what he said. I thought he was calling for another date. Why else would he be calling? But he was calling to tell me he'd had a great time, but he didn't think we were a match. It stung. Rejection doesn't feel good and it all sounded so cliched. But this was novel. *He actually called.* The others had not. He was calling to tell me how he felt, and he did it in a sensitive manner. I've always respected him for the courage it must have taken to pick up the phone and make that difficult call. If only all men were as brave as Cool&Kind.

Prayers for Our Seas to Split

This was all draining me. The only way to get married was to keep moving forward and trying, but I felt like giving up. In the middle of all these awful dates, an envelope was delivered from a Marine base. It was from AlmondEyes. My mother's eyebrows went up, but she didn't say anything. She gave me her I-hope-you-don't-do-anything-foolish look. And I gave her the I'm-so-excited-but-I-promise-I'm-not-doing-anything-foolish look back. I would open the letter in privacy and savor the words.

Each letter opened my eyes to foreign worlds. He had grown up in a military family. His father had fought in Korea and met his mother there. He was Amerasian but grew up in Oklahoma. It was like reading a good book, but in this case, I had met the author and the stories were real.

In turn, he was intrigued by my background as a Jew and child of Holocaust survivors. We asked and answered so many questions. This was captivating. It was not the dry interview questions I got on the dates. He was far away. I was safe.

I knew I was developing feelings for him. My guilt spurred me to be a better Jew. I started going to *shul* every Shabbos and prayed harder than ever. I persevered in my *parshah* studies each week. I took Torah classes in the city. I donated pints of blood at the hospital near our home. I wanted to do the right thing. Not just for my mother, but for myself, my soul, and my own relationship with God.

By donating, I was trying to make sense of life. I would rather be on the giving end, than the receiving end. I was told that one pint could save up to three lives. I had to do this. This was the easiest way for me to do something like save a life without risking my own on a battlefield. I thought of all the soldiers who had lost their lives, fighting to save my parents' lives during the war.

I had done nothing but write letters to a guy stuck on a ship or on base, but my feelings for him were growing and I felt guilty about that. I wasn't sure why. Because I was scaring or disappointing my mother? Because if anyone else knew they'd be disappointed too? Was my seventh-grade verse about Yochanan the High Priest haunting me? Or Chava from *Fiddler on the Roof*?

I was sure I would not run away with him. Was I too sure of myself? Every two months I went to donate blood. I wanted to do good with all my might. I studied *Tanach* more. Visited sick people too. I prayed harder. I wanted the right person to come to me, but were my letters drawing me further away from any possibility? AlmondEyes made me feel understood. When would someone with my own values do the same?

Intuitively, I recognized that going on a blind date was inherently unnatural and put people on edge, made the guys nervous compared to the way I met AlmondEyes. I tried to give my blind dates the benefit of the doubt. But those I hoped to see again rejected me, one by one.

She's too religious, too modern, too smart, too dumb, too tall, too short. Just like my father's *Too Too Twins* stories I had heard as a child. I wanted to marry a religiously observant man, and the Talmud says that matching couples is as difficult as the splitting of the Red Sea when the Jews left Egypt. I was gradually beginning to understand just how difficult it truly would be to meet my match and to comprehend the scope of the miracle needed. Most of my classmates had married, but so many other young women I had befriended in the intervening years at *Shabbatonim* or singles' events had not. *Was this a generational punishment, social consequence, or happenstance?* I added their names to my *Tehillim* list and prayed heartfelt pleas on behalf of us all – prayers for our seas to split.

Pulling Out All the Stops

One of my college friends was getting married. At the wedding, I sat at a table for singles when my friend leaned over and whispered, "I think I'm going to start asking guys out, as they never ask me."

Hmm, I thought, *perhaps I should do the same.*

I was tired of going to other people's weddings. I wanted to have my own. Then I realized that the guy sitting to my left was a prime candidate. I had known Seatmate for years from this group. He was a bit self-deprecating, but altogether a nice guy. *Why was I waiting to be asked?*

I whispered back, "Were you thinking of him?" and motioned to my left.

"No way," I read her lips, "he's all yours."

I had never had trouble talking to this fellow before, but I was suddenly tongue-tied. I did not want to ask him in public. I didn't want to put him on the spot, and most of all, I did not want to get rejected at a wedding, of all places. I poked my salad with my fork and made small talk with my friend, while I tried to think out my strategy.

Maybe in a few months, all of us could be back for our wedding! I hadn't even asked Seatmate out yet, and I was already daydreaming of our wedding. *Silly me, anyhow he would probably say no, wouldn't he? If he were interested, he would've already asked me!* As he hadn't, he was presumably not interested.

To save face – his and mostly mine – I mailed him a letter. That way he could crumple it up and toss it out and never say a word, and we could pretend it never happened. Yes, I must be a glutton for punishment because even weighed down with all my doubts, I wrote the letter. I spent more time on those twenty words than on most of my school reports because I had to get it just right, and nothing sounded right to me. Finally, I settled on, *"How do you feel about women asking men out? Because if you're okay with it, that's what I'm doing now."* I signed off with my phone number and dropped the letter in the mailbox.

See, God? Once again, I willingly set myself up for humiliation because I'm trying, really, really, really, hard. I hope You see that, God.

Days later, Seatmate called. He said he would love to go out with me. *Really?* I had been bracing myself for a "No." I was preparing to let a week or two go by before I bought a pint of ice cream or some other reward to assuage my pain. Now he had actually called? *Wow wee.* The wedding planning thoughts immediately resumed.

"You're not conning me, are you?" I asked.

"Why would I do a thing like that?"

"You really want to go out with me?"

"I wouldn't have called if I didn't. Besides I always thought you were very nice."

Hmm. There was something I was missing here, "I need to ask you something."

"Shoot."

"Why didn't you ever ask me out if you liked me?" I just didn't get it.

"Because you seemed like a popular girl who would say 'No' to me."

Huh. My jaw hung open and thank God he couldn't see that over the phone. He had that all wrong! I was desperate for dates, I had mostly lousy ones, and almost no one asked me out.

It was a watershed moment for me. I realized that perception and reality often don't mesh. The way he thought of me had taken me aback and was not at all what I thought of myself. Perhaps nothing was as it seemed and we all waste energy over figments of our own imagination. Maybe popular people were really insecure; haughty people are shy; and that happy couple we envy are simply two old friends glad to have run into each other again.

61

Seatmate and I went out for three weeks and I was open to seeing how things would progress. Then despite all his uplifting words, like all the other men, except for Cool&Kind, he took the coward's way out and dumped me without a word or explanation. It hurt, but I reminded myself it had little to do with me. It was cowardice – the inability to handle things maturely. I remained gracious and later set him up with a friend, despite all that. He eventually got engaged to the girl he met right after dating my suggestion. He didn't invite me to their wedding, even though I had remained gracious, even though I had set him up. Perhaps he felt uncomfortable inviting women. Nevertheless, I felt defeated.

In the meantime, my brother was finishing school and not ready to date. But he was being bombarded with potential matches. The phone rang all the time. People had nieces or friends with daughters or co-workers or neighbors who were all lovely girls, just as desperate for a date as my sister and I. Men had their pick, and even the worst of them were super sure they could get what they want. When it came to their wish lists, the sky was the limit. I did not feel that I had a long list of preferences. I just wanted someone Jewish I could talk to as easily as I could with AlmondEyes. But I did not meet that person.

I decided to mix things up a bit. I would put a classified ad in an Upper West Side flyer seeking a husband. It was used mainly for finding roommates or selling furniture. Was I a pathetic desperate woman to stoop to this level, or would the initiative open new avenues for me? Would men be intrigued or turned off? This was way before the internet, so the idea of meeting a random stranger this way seemed somewhat risky. However, the Jewish community's relatively small size made it easy to play Jewish geography, find out which synagogue the guy prayed in, and who his rabbi was.

I met with strangers all the time. I had met men in school, at singles' parties, and weekends. I had a chance to get a sense of them before accepting a date, true, but I would not know if they were hiding anything. The men matchmakers sent were equally risky. Most of the time, they weren't properly vetted. They told the matchmaker where they prayed or who their parents were, but did the matchmakers know if they had an arrest record? If they were in debt? If they were honest? Did the matchmakers meet them in person and truly engage with them or did they only speak briefly on the phone? Would the matchmaker know if they were hiding anything? I often found myself on a date with someone who was nothing like his description, yet he had my address, picked me up, and brought me home. Sometimes I did not feel comfortable in the car with some of these men, but I never felt truly endangered.

At times, I did receive and call references, but they would mostly say nice things about their friend, neighbor, congregant, or student. Very rarely had people given me information that truly mattered.

So now the classified ad was an experiment I was willing to take a chance on. It didn't seem riskier than anything else I had tried. In response to my ad, I received a lot of mail. Too many men did not write a word. They sent their phone numbers or their photos thinking that was sufficient to hook my interest. Some did take the time to write, but their grammar, spelling, and the contents of their letters were downright crummy. Others wrote their entire life story without knowing who they were writing to. One man wrote a decent letter, so we arranged to meet.

At first glance, he was clearly much older than me. Grandpa's hands had liver spots and I was recently out of college. *Did he lie about his age or did he leave it out?* I could not remember. Before we got into his car, I already wanted to leave, but I did not want to be rude so decided to make the best of it. Then Grandpa said he was so happy about this date and he needed to confide in me. *Of course, he's thrilled, I'm young enough to be his granddaughter!* I thought he would confess that he was decades older than me. "Well, what is it you'd like to tell me?"

"I wanted you to hear this from me first." *OK, this is not gonna be good.* "Because I was accused of rape, but I didn't do it."

My mind went blank. I didn't feel afraid, but what an ice breaker! *Who uses this as an opening line? Who talks like that? And who gets stuck on a date with a guy who talks like that? Only pathetic me.*

My thoughts turned to God and the concept of *hishtadlus*, of doing my part so that God does His. *I lowered myself to putting a classified ad in after all my other efforts failed – and I find myself in a car with an alleged rapist? Sigh. I just want to go home. Now.* But I said all the right things and did what I could to get the date over with as soon as possible, with as much grace as possible.

Nice or Not

I was set up with a nice guy who hunched over and seemed to shrink into his jacket. We met after work at a restaurant of his choice. I had never been there before, so I was glad to try out a new place. But I had not realized how expensive it would be. He was Nice, but a "how many sisters and brothers" grill interviewer, like many others. I was dreadfully uninterested in being interviewed yet again. But unlike many others, Nice was not cheap. In fact, he was extravagant and this restaurant had been his choice.

I was not comfortable when a date was cheap, but equally uncomfortable when too much was spent on me, especially if I was doubtful about wanting a second date. I didn't want to owe anyone a second date, or let down a man after he had been so generous. I searched for the cheapest entrées on the menu, but there were none. I felt trapped, waited till he ordered his entrée, then ordered mine – feeling very wicked because I was close to sure I wouldn't want another date.

I was still learning to assert myself and stop dating someone just to please the matchmaker. I didn't have strength to make meaningless small talk with a countless number of men, but it required equal strength to say no to a second try. Sometimes I caved in to a second date, but that made the inevitable rejection harder. I was learning slowly.

This time, I was determined to say "no." But Nice made it hard. Instead of escorting me to the subway as others did when we met in the city after work, he ordered a cab. This meant more money, more time, and a stilted conversation overheard by a cabdriver. Very painful.

When we got to my home, he reached to open his door. I told him he needn't make the cabdriver wait, and I would be fine. He insisted on escorting me to the door. He was following every rule in the rule book perfectly, but he was missing the cues I was sending out. He was being a perfect gentleman however, nice or not, I was incredibly uncomfortable with him. I was certain I was not going to marry this man. It distressed me to hurt him, but I could not and would not be convinced to give him a second shot, despite the protestations of the matchmaker. There was no flicker of any connection between us – intellectually, emotionally, conversationally. Nice is far better than not nice. But nice is not enough. If I weren't sure, maybe I'd try again. But, I'm sure. *I'm sorry. No. Just no!*

At the other extreme were those who took me to dinner, yet wanted a cheap date. There's plenty to do that is fun and free. We could visit Central Park, go to a museum on its free night, go biking. It just required imagination. I didn't need or want a blind date to spend money on me, but being noticeably cheap is another matter entirely. A few of these frugal guys took me to nice restaurants, but limited my order to a side dish.

One guy rang my bell. When I opened the door, I saw a man wearing a messenger bag leaning on his bike. He was my date.

"Um, I'm not really sure what to do with my bike," he said. I wasn't sure either. Did Biker hope I would hop on? *What did the matchmaker say he did? Was he a messenger? Did he earn a living?* Oh drat! My neighbors were passing by and staring. I was in a hurry to scram out of there.

"Can I come upstairs and call a car service?" he asked.

No way, Jose! You should have thought of that before you hopped on your bike to get here. But all I said was, "Let's lock your bike here, and walk to the nearest kosher place." I just wanted to get away from the onlookers. We walked to the first decent place and it was a medium-priced restaurant. We sat down, looked over the menu, and he said he couldn't afford the meals. I bristled in silence and continued to stare at the menu. *Why hadn't he planned where we would go or how we'd get there ahead of time? He was just too shiftless.*

"Why don't you order a soup?" he said.

Something – perhaps the public stares I had just endured standing next to this hapless fellow in full view of my neighbors – made me snap. Ordering a soup meant avoiding an entrée. I had been humiliated this way one time too many. "Sorry! I am not a soup kind of girl!"

I was not nice and knew it. I was angry. Angry at Biker. Angry at God. Angry at my neighbors – a nice couple who had set me up with him. Were they nice or not?

The waitress came over and Biker gave her our order: "I'd like one entrée for both of us to share."

And I'd like to order the power of invisibility.

She sighed, looked pointedly at him and said, "There is a minimum of one entrée per person during dinner hours." He turned beet red, ordered another entrée, but mortification had destroyed my appetite.

Doctored Up

One year I decided to join a hotel group for Rosh Hashanah, a departure from my usual custom of spending the holidays with my family. I was seated at a table with several nice couples and at the end of the weekend, one of wives told me she had met a friend in medical school who was single. Would I have been wrong to assume that this man would be as appealing as all of the married men at that table? Should I have not trusted this woman? Yes and no.

It was a Sunday afternoon and my neighbors were all out, sitting on their porches and stoops about to witness a pathetic show. A rickety dented van pulled up in front of my house. A man with a messy beard, stained pants, and *tzitzis* dangling beneath his untucked shirt got out of the back of the van and rang my bell. *He looks like a beggar, not a doctor. Oh my! Oh my!* I was already markedly disappointed and uncomfortable, but as I neared the van with tinted windows, the back door slid open and I saw what appeared to be an entire family in that van.

"Who are these people?" I asked Doc. I was agitated that my neighbors had front-row seats to this drama.

"They're my friends. I told them I need a ride and they offered to help pick you up."

If they were truly his friends, wouldn't they have told Doc it's unacceptable to pick up a date alongside an entire family? That it simply was not appropriate?

"Um, no. I'm not getting into that van. Sorry," I said. *This is ridiculous and awfully embarrassing. I can't believe this is my life. I'm ready to quit. Quit. Do You hear me? Did that lady doctor truly think I would go for this schlemiel? Would she?*

"Then what should we do?" he asked, completely flummoxed. Another hapless fellow in my life.

My mind was racing. I was ready to end the date right here and right now. *I needed to scram out of there real quick before all my neighbors witnessed one more moment of this sorry episode.* "We are going to walk to the corner and find our own car service," I said as I walked off with him stumbling after me.

I whizzed right past the car service on the corner. I couldn't imagine getting into any car with this man. I didn't want the driver to look at the two of us as a couple or overhear what was sure to be another inane conversation like the many I'd already endured. I kept walking. Doc kept talking. But my thoughts crowded him out.

How could she think I'd feel comfortable with this person? How could she think he was comparable in any way to her husband or any of the other husbands at the table? Why hadn't she warned me? Why had she done this to me? What in the world was she THINKING? Was she thinking at all? I'm better off not dating. I'm ready to join a convent. Very funny.

I couldn't be nice to this man. He had unwittingly shamed me in front of all my neighbors. I tried to be civil. I knew they knew it was a blind date and that I wasn't "with" him. But still. Years of being humiliated this way had taken its toll.

I could not say "This too is for the good." *Gam zu l'tova.* Not for the millionth time. I was too angry. At the woman. At the world. At God. I could not stand another moment of this. After twelve blocks of racing. I stopped.

"I haven't seen a car service yet," he said. "What are we gonna do?" We had in fact scooted past several, but he had been oblivious.

"We are going to walk back because I'm feeling unwell," I said. That was definitely true.

I prayed my neighbors had disappeared by then. We walked all the way back to the car service on my corner where he ordered a car home. I didn't want him to escort me to my door. I slunk home slowly, making sure no one would see me. Fortunately, they had all gone in.

Years later, I saw Doc hanging out aimlessly at corner bodegas along with homeless bums. It was hard to imagine him in medical school at all. I thought about our matchmaker. Had he been perfectly normal when she knew him? How many years had passed since she had seen him? Did she know what had become of him? Had she deliberately doctored him up? I didn't know, and I didn't care. I was too bummed.

Till East Meets West

My Jewish co-workers at this time were secular. They did not think I was smart in being so rigid in my choice of husband. One elderly woman admitted she was married to a Jewish man, "but it was pure chance, I really didn't care," she told me. Though her kids were Jewish, they had intermarried.

One of my bosses was a secular Israeli who took pride in my observance. The guys in the studio told me he had warned them the day before I started, "Guys, you better clean up your language. We have a religious girl starting tomorrow."

He was understanding and flexible about my schedule, early Fridays and Jewish holidays. I had friendly religious debates with him every now and then. One day, he called me into his office and dropped the folded *NY Times* onto his desk and pointed to the article on the page. "Now take a look at that. There's a matchmaker in LA for observant Jews. You should call her, broaden your horizons to the west coast. I want to see you get married." At this point, I'd had my fill of matchmakers and felt resistant to calling yet another one all the way on the west coast. But he followed up with me, as a mother hen would, and so I dutifully called her.

A few days later, a gentleman she had suggested called me. West sounded pleasant but lived out west. He ended the call by saying that when he visits the east coast, he'd give me a call. I was okay with that. I didn't want months of long-distance calls without meeting in person.

Several months later, I was at a wedding and sitting at a singles' table, chatting with a fellow who seemed completely enamored with me. I was growing accustomed to the fact that men were either very interested in me or not at all. A few days after the wedding, the new bride called to tell me her friend, East, had asked about me. He had been too shy to ask me for my number, but could he have it? I was happy to say he could.

He didn't call.

It took a few months till East finally gathered his nerve to call me. By then, I had given up hope of ever hearing from him. I was pleasantly surprised, especially as it was a Sunday morning, which seemed like an odd time to call a date. But we chatted and made plans to meet later that week. Half an hour after hanging up with East, the phone rang again. This time it was West, whom I had spoken to six months earlier. How strange. One had my number for nearly half a year and the other for several months and they both chose to call me on a Sunday morning only a half hour apart. This is so odd. *God has a sense of humor.* I had not had any dates in months, and now it seemed I would have two in the span of a week. I preferred to focus on each man one at a time and give him my full attention, rather than juggle two or more men and compare and contrast. But this is how it worked out. They both seemed worth meeting.

West was telling me about his plans to come to New York this week and I casually asked him where he stayed when he came to our city. Did he have relatives in the area? I tugged at the spiral phone cord and twined it around my finger, "No," he responded, "I have a friend, East, I stay at when I visit."

I let go of the cord. It snapped and bounced back into place. "Did you say East? What's his last name?"

It was the very same East that I had just made a date with a short while ago. I groaned. What were the chances of something like this happening? *God, You are way too funny.* This was not good. East was very liable to ask West about his date with a New York girl.

I had to tell them the truth. West was not happy. "Why did you make a date with him, if you knew I was calling?" *Huh? He was supposed to call six months ago! Did he really think that I would not date anyone while waiting? I had no assurances he would ever call.* He argued that he had "first dibs" on me since he spoke to me first. It was ridiculously immature. I gave him the option of bowing out but said I would not cancel a date I had already made just to suit him. He opted to make a date.

Both West and East met me that week. They spent their entire time with me voicing their displeasure about my date with the other. Neither of them tried to make the best of the situation and live in the moment. It was a disaster, as I was stuck between these squabbling competitors. Our dates had gone south.

Train of Thought

One day, after work, I window-shopped till my legs grew tired. I was hoping for a seat on the subway, but did not get one. I leaned against the door when I spotted a cute guy with a *kippah*. He was the type that never gave me a second glance, except that this one did. I didn't know if he was just looking, or *looking*. I wasn't sure, but I didn't want to think about it. I assumed he was married and turned around.

Two stops later, when the subway pulled into the station, a woman next to the door stood up to leave, so I sat down and saw Look was still looking, but he also walked toward a seat further down. Now I was sure he had been *looking*. I was always a bit taken aback when I got what I felt was undeserved attention. We were both sitting on the same side, so I couldn't get a clear view of him. At every stop, I turned to look in his direction to see him disembark, but he didn't. Surely, he couldn't be going to my area in Brooklyn. My curiosity grew.

Then I saw his arms go up above his head in a dramatic stretch and he leaned forward and turned in my direction. He was most definitely leaning over to look right at me. *Why was he looking at me? Who was he? Gee, I wish I could talk to him.* As the subway passed station after station and he did not get off, I was certain he was going to my area, but where would he get off? Was he going to visit someone? See a doctor? Shop? Or did he live here? I wanted to know!

We were two stops away from my stop and he didn't get off. *I should ask him something, anything, the time, directions, um anything.* But my mouth was dry and my heart was pounding. One stop away, and he didn't get off! I stood up and walked to the door a few minutes before we reached my stop. I was getting off soon and hadn't said a word. I was not a shy person – what the heck was the matter with me? I would get off and that would be that. Then I saw him get up too. My stop? This was unreal.

Was he my neighbor? I had never seen him before. He was probably just visiting. He stood two inches away and my heart was pounding. *Say something!* But I didn't and neither did he. My tongue felt dry and chalky. He turned his head and I saw a name knitted on his *kippah* on the back of his head. I savored the sound of it. Was that his name on the *kippah*, or had he borrowed a friend's? The subway pulled into the stop, the doors slid open and we both walked out – each of us very consciously "not" looking – trying to act casual – feeling anything but. I was rendered completely speechless, which my family would call miraculous. Once we descended the stairs from the elevated platforms, I went one way and he went the other. *Oh God! That was my husband who just walked away!* I was sure of it! I was delusional.

I went home and told my family what had happened, even though clearly nothing had happened. Then I called three friends to repeat the story of my lost chance at eternal happiness. I went to bed and cried all night. I acted as though a long-lasting romance had ended and shattered me to pieces. Nothing had happened. He just looked at me. *What was wrong with me? Was it our eye contact and unspoken language? Or had desperation made me go off the deep end?* I lay in bed plotting how to find him. I was almost sure of his first name and I knew which stop he had gotten off. Perhaps I could do something with that information.

I would make up signs saying "Is your name 'Look'? I saw you on the subway last night. Please contact me at...." and then I would post them all over that subway station. Excited about my plan and unable to sleep in any case, I left my house earlier than usual so I could work on the signs in the office and paste them all over the station when I returned home that evening. It didn't occur to me how absurd my idea was or that strangers might call me just for kicks. I was in a frenzy to reach him. I would probably come to my senses and see the folly of my idea before the day was over, but as I approached the station, I could not believe my eyes.

I saw him. Again! Two days in a row, and I had never seen him before. Perhaps he had recently moved or left early every day and so we had never crossed paths before. It had clearly not been a doctor's appointment. He probably lives here.

He was speaking to another man with a *kippah* and they both passed through the turnstiles and bolted up the stairs to the platform without seeing me. *I cannot repeat my mistake of last night. I don't know what I'm going to say, but I'm going to say something. After my night of mourning, I'm definitely not going to let this opportunity slip away again.* I climbed the stairs and when I got to the platform, I saw the back of his leather jacket further down. He was talking to the other man who now noticed my approach. I slowed down. The other man looked at me in confusion over Look's shoulder. Look turned around. He recognized me and smiled. I smiled back. "I saw you on the train last night," I said, praying he didn't hear my knees knock.

"I saw you too," he said. Then he introduced me to his roommate and told me he lived in the area. We chatted the entire way. He was very smooth and slick. He'd had plenty of practice talking to women. Then he asked me if I wanted to meet that night. That was quick, but *yes, oh yes,* I did. He had captivated me.

We met and talked and talked and walked and walked, and he was generous and handsome and interesting and dreamy, the complete opposite of so many of the others like Biker or Grandpa. When I found out he was younger than me, I was astonished. He seemed mature beyond his years, well-educated, well-spoken, well-mannered, and well-traveled. He had lived in several places, clearly had his wits about him, and more. He even dressed well and had every hair in place. And, oh yes, he complimented me very much and I enjoyed hearing those compliments, even if I didn't quite believe them.

The only thing that made me uneasy was his perfection. I was scared something would go wrong like all the other times I had liked someone. He seemed too good to be true. *Could it finally be happening for me?* Yes. He asked me out again at the end of the date. So, late at night, while trying to sleep, I was talking to God. A lot. Thanking Him. Praising Him. Telling Him I owed him big time.

Look and I went out every day. It was a whirlwind romance. We talked about everything – our pasts, our dreams and hopes. He had not grown up observant and he spoke about his path to observance and his belief in God. Once again, my mother pulled out her well-worn warning, "Be careful, I don't want you to get hurt. Take your time. Do you really need to see him every day?" But Look was like a crystal glass of clean, crisp, cold, clear water appearing in a dry, parched, hot, sunny desert. I had been trudging in that desert for a long time and was thirsty for this. I didn't want my mother to worry, but I needed this. If I did get hurt, it wouldn't be the first time. I had to see this through.

I wanted to see where he lived, so for our next date, I walked over to his address. It was not far. In fact, I knew the house and his landlady. His roommate, a pleasant fellow, was there, but I was there for Look.

He showed me around the apartment and then his room.

Then he made a pass at me.

I thought of Whiskers and how turned off I was. And Jr.Engineer – well that had been a goodbye. Yet Look was someone I was very attracted to, but I wanted to have a kosher relationship. I wanted to do things properly. We were not supposed to touch each other. We were not supposed to be alone. I thought *yeshivish* guys would perhaps never forgive me for the Whiskers and Jr.Engineer episodes, but this guy would because of his own history.

But now I worried about the opposite extreme. Would he forgive me for wanting to keep the proper boundaries? Was this all he wanted? *Oh no*, he said. *I admire you and that's exactly what I like about you.* So! He respected my boundaries. We spoke to his roommate and looked at photo albums and then he asked me out for the following Sunday.

He picked me in the morning and we spent the entire day together. We strolled around and people-watched in Central Park, had a picnic lunch that he had prepared, visited the conservatory gardens. We went out for dinner in a fancy restaurant and when dinner was done, he went up to the counter and had some food boxed. I figured it was his dinner for tomorrow.

"Would you like to go to a movie?" he asked. It would take us at least another hour to get home with the subway, so I would get home by 10:00 pm, at the earliest. By then, it would've been an eleven-hour date. A movie would prolong it another few hours.

I'd had enough for one day. I was exhausted and had to go to work the next day. I also had to consider my parents who would be concerned, as I still lived at home with them. "Oh, come on!" he said. But I had my limits.

He was upset, but relented. We were quiet on the way home. Just before we parted, he handed me the box tied in string, "This is for you and your parents."

"Isn't this your food for tomorrow?"

"No. I bought you a present."

I was over the moon. I thanked him and went in to my parents who asked me where I could've possibly been on an eleven-hour date? They were upset that I had spent so much time with him.

"Listen, I'm an adult and I didn't do anything wrong! If I were nineteen and married as my classmates are, I wouldn't have to tell you my schedule! He gave me something for you."

I handed them the box. Inside was a perfect blueberry pie. My parents were still concerned, but that had been my perfect dream date. I hoped it would lead to marriage.

And then.

Then.

It was like all the other times.

He didn't call again. I was stupefied and I *knew* it all at the same time. It *was* too good to be true, too perfect. I had been a fool for love. I had never "fallen" for someone so immediately and so quickly. It was all too "cute" – when does anyone meet a significant someone on the subway?

And so, my train of thought began. An eleven-hour date, and then nothing? Was he mad that I didn't go to the movie? That I opted to be *shomer negiah*? Or had he died in an accident? No. No. None of the others had died in an accident, when I desperately sought to give them the benefit of the doubt. They were all alike. Cowards. He was just another coward. Was he a heartless soul? A user? A liar? A con? I would never be certain, and never ever wanted to date again. It would take time to nurse this wounded heart. And a long, long time for that train of thought to stop.

Credit Crunch

I was being more careful vetting my dates ahead of time. I didn't want to spend countless evenings with stranger after stranger having inane conversations. I could not bear it. The opportunities to meet men on my own were dwindling, so I pushed myself to go to singles' weekends, lectures, and events with my friends. More often than not, we would befriend new women, but still come home without having been asked out by any men.

Finally at one lecture, a very nice down to earth guy did ask me out. He seemed to be a solid guy, tall – and yes, handsome – but not in the slick, suave too-good-to-be-true-way that Look had been. I would not allow someone's "polish" to blind me to his character again. I wanted someone substantive, reliable and solid that I could marry.

I still felt twinges of guilt for the things I had done or come close to doing. I blamed myself and it affected my self-esteem. I felt remorse and sullied by those events. I resolved to put them behind me and focus on the future. I would put my best foot forward on my upcoming date.

I didn't have the usual pre-date anxiety of who he would turn out to be as I had met him at a party. I also did not pre-plan my fantasy wedding. Solid and I went to a restaurant whose ambiance was quiet and dignified. For the first time in a long time, things felt "normal." It was not an awkward, uncomfortable date and it was not too good to be true. There was the tentative getting to know you feeling coupled with an easy flow of conversation. It was exactly as any normal first date should be. We had a pleasant dinner. The waitress came over with the bill and Solid handed her his credit card.

"We don't accept credit cards here, sir," she said. "Cash only."

I could read the discomfort in his face. Neither of us expected a restaurant not to accept a credit card. Apparently, he did not have enough cash on him but I didn't fault him for that. However, I did have cash. "I can help out."

"Uh… no it's okay. Actually, uh, maybe I'd better… We'll find an ATM when we leave."

"Sure, no problem. We couldn't have known. It's really fine." I handed him the bills and I could sense his discomfort. There was no need for it and I truly did not mind. I tried my best to make light of it, but clearly his frame of mind had taken a turn for the worse.

We left the restaurant and he was on a mission to find the nearest ATM. He could barely look at me. I just followed his lead. I was not sure if anything I could say would help or hurt the matter. We finally found an ATM from which he withdrew cash and handed some over. Admittedly, the whole episode felt a bit unsavory. It cheapened our experience, and deep down inside I realized the gratuitous shame of this moment would probably prevent him from calling me again. I felt desolate at the wasted opportunity and wondered how our date would've turned out had they accepted his card. Did my entire future hinge on a random stroke of bad luck or was God orchestrating events?

Sometimes I wasn't sure at all. Though we had met on our own, which meant he liked me enough to ask me out, my intuition was correct. I never heard from Solid again.

Only You Can

I was growing despondent. *What do I do, God? You know I gave up writing to AlmondEyes despite my urge to continue. I didn't want to waste my time, and certainly not his. I didn't want to do the wrong thing and am working hard to do the right thing. Please help me to do Your Will. To marry someone Jewish. To build a Jewish home. Only You can.*

Months went by and I was trying to refocus on the positive aspect of the men I was meeting. I had heard about the tile syndrome. One can walk into a room tiled with a thousand tiles and if one tile was missing, the eye would be drawn to what was missing, instead of what was there. *Was I guilty of that? Was I judging men for the one thing they lacked rather than everything else they offered? I resolved to try not to do that.* As much as I recognized when a man was nice or kind, if I didn't feel I could be myself with him, if I didn't feel our personalities or interests were anywhere in the same ballpark, if I didn't feel I could develop a friendship, was I expected to force things and marry him?

Some people offered guidance. "Oh, you'll be so busy when you're married; you'll talk about the kids, you won't need to share interests!" or "Compatibility is overrated." None of their advice seemed sound to me and I wondered whether they were happy. Didn't I deserve as much? Or if they were not, did they expect me to follow suit? Had they married young? Could they comprehend what I'd been through? Mostly I didn't want advice that felt like judgment. I wanted them to introduce me to men. But those who gave unsolicited advice freely, very rarely came up with a date suggestion.

There were others who were sensitive and knew that single women were not overly picky. They saw the situation for what it was. They knew that as difficult as dating was for men, the odds were stacked against women. These sympathetic people were generous with their time and their encouragement, and they worked hard to come up with good suggestions. But the pool of eligible men was shrinking. As much as they helped, God was in control, and I needed His help more than theirs.

So, I prayed again and again. *Please help me to do Your Will. To marry someone Jewish. To build a Jewish home. Only You can.*

Out of Order

God chose to help my brother instead. My younger brother had lists of potential dates before he ever started dating. He had gone out with several girls during the course of a year. As soon as one girl broke his heart, another one was lined up. My sister and I were not surprised because we had seen the flurry of calls. From his stories, I gathered that most of my brother's dates were pleasant. He was very sensitive to his two older sisters. He asked us how we felt about him dating, he told us when his relationship got serious, and even let us try on the engagement ring. In turn, we gave him tips on courtship, and helped plan his marriage proposal.

My mother whose shoulder I had cried on, who was always there for us, supported us through this emotional time. Even my father, who was often baffled and frustrated by his daughters' disinterest in all the men he dug up for us, held his questions in check.

My brother and parents didn't make us feel over the hill or spinsterish, but plenty of others unwittingly managed to make us feel just that way with their pitying looks or comments. "Nu, when is it your turn? After all, you're no spring chicken." As though I needed their reminder that I was getting older. They all said "*Im Yirtzeh Hashem,* God willing, your turn will come too," which is well meaning. Still, when one hears that for the thousandth time, it doesn't sound sweet any longer. It was beginning to grate on my nerves. *God willing this and God willing that. Obviously, God was not willing.* Or did they think that *I* was not willing?

Nevertheless, I felt beautiful at my brother's wedding. My hair was styled and highlighted; my makeup was done; the silver gown I wore glittered and made me feel glamorous. I wouldn't let anyone ruin this night for me. As I marched down the aisle towards my brother's *chuppah*, I was grateful that one of us was getting married. And I hoped someday my sister and I would walk down our own aisles to our own *chuppos*.

You

Throughout it all, You have been there, God. *Thank God. God willing. Oh God.* Most of all, day in and day out I've reached out to You in one way or another. I praise you. *Hallelukah.* I thank you. *Hodu L'Hashem.* I cry to You. *God help me.* Pray to You. *Blessed Are You God, My God.* Beg You. *Ad anah, Hashem?* I've made an awful lot of deals with You as though puny little me has the power to change Your Almighty mind. I know I can't trick You into giving me what I want, nevertheless, I try because I'll try anything. You're not Santa Claus or a vending machine, but I keep drawing up my lists and putting metaphorical quarters in.

I've said *Perek Shira, Shir Hashirim,* Psalms, joined *Tehillim* groups, done midnight *segulos* and even ran to *mekubalim.* And while none of it has yielded me a spouse, and all of it felt like an attempt to trick You, something did change. I developed a deeper relationship with You. I came to know You through a different lens. I surrendered to You.

I've learned that when people tell me I will get married, *Im Yirtzeh Hashem,* if You, God will it, then there is the possibility that You, God do not will it. That it cannot be *Your* will only if I marry, and *my* fault if I don't. You are always in charge – not just when one's fortune is good.

There is no figuring You out. You're too, too great. If Moshe could not see You, neither can I. If Yonah could not escape You, neither can I. If Iyov cannot comprehend Your ways, neither can I. If millions can suffer in the world, with illness, poverty, war, cruelty, starvation, and massacres, there is no reason I should not undergo my share that pales in comparison to theirs.

We're taught that we are not subject to the laws of nature – that our prayers – and most of all, our actions, via *mitzvos* – can change our destiny. The course of our fate can be affected by our mind, heart, words, and actions. If we seek to be a better Jew and fulfill our soul's yearning to get closer to You, we can perhaps indeed shake the heavens. Perhaps not. We cannot control You, but we can learn to recognize that we must control ourselves instead. That is all we can do. That, and stand in awe of You.

PART THREE

How Long Will You Hide Your Countenance (Psalms 13:2)

עד אנא תסתר את פניך (תהילים י"ג:ב)

Jackpot

I had finally hit the jackpot. Well, not exactly. Every now and then, I met someone nice that was not my match. I'd then try to see if I knew anyone for him. I had drawn up lists of singles and had a group of friends do the same so we could mix and match, but nothing had come of it. However, one time I did make a match at last.

Four *Shabbatonim* I'd attended led to this one match. Even though it was not me who got married, as the go-between for the couple who did, I felt I had won the jackpot.

I went to *Shabbaton* #1 where I met Fixer, who lived on the Upper West Side. After the weekend, she fixed me up with a guy she knew from the West Side crowd, Chosson-to-Be. After our dinner, he walked me to the subway. The West Side guys didn't usually have cars, so I met them after work in the city. Very often, they'd just wave me off when leaving the restaurant. Some would walk me to the nearest subway station and *then* wave me off. But Chosson-to-Be came down into the station with me, swiped his Metrocard for me and entered the station so he could wait on the platform with me for my train. He was a mensch.

Before the train arrived, he asked me for a second date. I hadn't expected that, as we were at different observance levels. I'd also thought he would go back to Fixer who had set us up. But as he was very amiable, I was willing to get to know him, and I accepted.

He didn't call.

I was disappointed, but he must've had second thoughts and realized we weren't a match after all. I was getting used to rejection and it had been just one date, so I moved on.

At *Shabbaton* #2 Chosson-to-Be was there. He had seen me, but averted his eyes as though he had not. He was probably very uncomfortable. But I did not want us to spend the entire day avoiding each other. He had been a mensch on our date, so I went right up to him and said, "Good Shabbos, how are you?"

He seemed relieved that I hadn't started shouting "Why didn't you call?" – that I let bygones be bygones. After that, whenever we saw each other, we had no difficulty speaking. I had chosen to be gracious about his rejection.

I took the bus to *Shabbaton* #3 from the city. After a few stops, a young lady, Kallah-to-Be, sat down in the seat next to me and we began to chat. I told her I was going to a weekend event and she told me she was going to her parents. She also told me she had become religious, had lived in Israel for a year, and had recently returned to the States. Our talk turned to dating. "I'm just not comfortable with the idea of matchmakers. I never needed them before."

"Then why don't you try a *Shabbaton?*"

"Oh no, no. Those are not for me either."

Well then, good luck to you. She was attractive and educated, but so were many women. Meeting someone was difficult. If one didn't put in effort – *hishtadlus* – nothing was bound to happen. We were always told how important *hishtadlus* was. That if we did our part, God would do His.

Later, I thought about this young woman, and Chosson-to-Be came to mind. Something about her reminded me of him, but I didn't have her phone number or her last name. I had thought of it too late. Months later, the idea still niggled at me and wouldn't let go. By this time, I had Chosson-to-Be's phone number and had invited him to several singles' *Melave Malkas* and social events I had organized. I set him up a few times too.

I started asking people everywhere whether they knew anyone named Kallah-to-Be. No one seemed to know her. She had lived in Israel until recently and before that, she hadn't been in religious circles. I kept searching for her.

I attended *Shabbaton* #4. It was being held at a synagogue in Queens and when I looked up from my prayer book, I saw her across the sanctuary. I froze and could no longer concentrate on my *davening*. As soon as prayers were over, I raced to catch her before she left the room.

"Good Shabbos! Do remember me?"

"Oh, hi! Of course!"

"How are you? I've been looking for you for months."

"You have?"

"Yes, and I'm so glad you finally signed up for a *Shabbaton*."

"I didn't! I told you I don't like them."

"Then what are you doing here?"

"This is my *shul*. I live here."

"Well, whatever you do, don't leave without giving me a way to reach you."

After their first date, Chosson-to-Be called to tell me it was "the best date he'd ever had." It took Kallah-to-Be a little longer to come around. But they ended up getting married.

God is in charge. This is a story of a guy who didn't call when he said he would, a girl who refused to go to single events, and an idea I couldn't shake out of my head, despite not knowing either of them very well. He was a guy I had one date with and she was a girl I met on a bus ride. This marriage was a miracle and I was God's messenger, that much I knew. Surely, I was a step closer to my own miracle.

Or was I?

Several months after their marriage, they took me out to dinner to thank me for making the match. During the course of the conversation, my single status came up. They had tried to reciprocate and set me up, but their suggestions had proven unproductive. Chosson declared blind dating ineffective. "Nobody ever meets a spouse on blind dates," he stated with conviction.

"Chosson!" Kallah exclaimed incredulously. She pointed to me, "*She* set us up! We met *because* of her and we're here to thank her for that!"

Oops. We all laughed. Their courtship and engagement had taken time and now, after months of marriage, they were completely at ease with each other. So much time had elapsed, he had apparently forgotten how it all began, even during the very meal where they were thanking their matchmaker.

Blind dating can be ineffective or even disastrous. On the other hand, it can result in happy marriages, as it did in their case – and I hoped, sometime soon, in mine.

For You Were Strangers in the Land

I had met Kallah on my bus ride to a *Shabbaton*. A nice young man had put it together. He was inexperienced, though well meaning. Unfortunately, only fifteen people had signed up and were mismatched in age and were at different observance levels. Nobody seemed to be a match for anyone else. We were all put up in people's homes, and when I first arrived, I heard I would be staying in the home of a very proactive community matchmaker. If there were no men to meet at the *Shabbaton*, perhaps she would be another networking avenue to pursue.

The home looked like a mansion from the outside. Inside, there was a foyer with a cathedral ceiling and gleaming marble floors, as well as a winding staircase that led to the second floor. The hostess directed me to the living room that looked like a page out of *Architectural Digest* and told me I would sleep on the convertible couch. I was surprised – in a home this huge – were there no guest bedrooms with more privacy? But she didn't offer any. I had often slept on lumpy mattresses in cold basements, humid attics, and cluttered kids' rooms, yet even in this mansion, I would be subjected to sleeping on a couch. I handed her a box of fresh bakery pastries I had picked up earlier.

As I unpacked my things, I heard a loud shriek from the kitchen. I ran into the foyer and she was standing there at the opened door. "You… you… what did you bring into my home? Take that box out of here right now. Take it outside!" and she pointed to the bakery box on the kitchen counter, I had handed her moments ago.

I was shaken by her screeching, and puzzled. I stepped into her all-white, pristine kitchen and went to the box. It was crawling with ants. I was astounded as I had bought it just hours ago at a bakery. But I was also humiliated by this woman. Was her shrieking necessary? She could have discreetly thrown it out and told me the truth without acting like it was my fault. Did she really believe I intended to bring in a box of ants? Is this the woman I had heard was a do-gooder, a volunteer, a pillar of the community, known to help people?

Another guest arrived, and our hostess led us both to her living room saying we would share the couch. By this time, I had found out that all of her children, except one, were gone for the summer. There were empty bedrooms upstairs and she wanted me to share a couch with a stranger? When was the last time she shared a bed with someone she did not know? I was not comfortable with this idea, but I was not bold enough to ask the woman for a bedroom. So, I hoped she would get the hint when I spoke up. "Do you have a spare blanket? I'm going to put it on the floor and sleep on that. I cannot share a bed with someone I don't know. Sorry."

She chose not to understand. "Sure, I'll bring one down for you," she said, in her benevolent tone. She had regained her equilibrium after I threw out the ant-infested box of pastries. She was the ultimate hostess. Of course, she could give me another blanket. Of course, I could sleep on the floor, even though there were four or five empty bedrooms upstairs. Why not?

My family would give up our own beds in our small apartment to make guests comfortable, and this woman who was well-known in her community for her generosity and good deeds was going to have her guest sleep on the floor?

The arrangement of this *Shabbaton* was that two single men would join two single women at their host's home on Friday night. On Shabbos day all the singles would gather and eat lunch at the synagogue. I had felt so fortunate that I would eat a meal at this generous soul's house and have a chance to acquaint myself with her, but now that I knew what this woman's true colors were, I dreaded it. Her husband, her mother, and one daughter sat with us four singles at their beautiful, candlelit Shabbos table. I tried to enjoy the meal and the rest of the company. The conversation was a bit superficial and I did not feel like joining in, but then my roommate chirped up. "How come people don't want to date converts?" Though thirty-six passages of the Torah enjoin us to be kind to converts, segments of religious society are prejudiced against them. From the little I knew of this family, I guessed that this topic was not a very good one for their table.

The hostess said coyly, "Well… who one marries is a very personal decision."

"But how can people decide they won't marry a convert if they don't even give them a chance?" she persisted.

"Um… ah… can you pass that salad please?" They steered the conversation in a different direction. I stayed out of it. The two men who were sitting with us were not at all suitable for me or the other woman in any way. I was glad when dinner was over.

Before going to sleep (on the floor, mind you), my roommate disclosed that she was a convert and had trouble getting dates. I told her that my friends and I had trouble getting dates as well, so I didn't know how much her conversion played into her difficulty. There were people, such as our hosts, who would unfortunately never give converts a chance, and she shouldn't waste energy getting into it with them.

The next day, we gathered at the synagogue to pray and then eat lunch. There were just a few people. Only one man in the room appeared to be in my age range as well as close to my observance level. I chatted a bit with him. After the meal, my roommate asked, "Were you interested in anyone at lunch?"

"Well one guy..."

"Was it the guy in the gray suit and hat?" she asked. "I saw you talking to him."

"Yeah. He seemed bright and he's nice looking."

She was quick to dismiss him. "Oh, you're not going to want to go out with him,"

"What makes you say that? In fact, he's the one guy this entire weekend that I would want to know better."

"Because he converted. He's a *ger!*"

"Wait a minute, he's a convert? He told me he's a *baal teshuvah* and that he didn't grow up religious. So how do you know?"

"Converts all know each other."

"Why do you think I wouldn't go out with him? Because now I'm even more interested. He's clearly a special man as you are a special woman. Don't write him off for me – you just told me yourself how hard it is for converts to get dates!"

"You're an FFB. *Frum*-from-birth people never want to date converts!"

I told her that while I could not speak for others, I would be honored to date a convert. Would others shun someone like our forefather Abraham, who discovered God on his own? I would not. Would others perhaps overlook Ruth, who chose Judaism over her own heritage? Her great-grandson was King David, who is destined to be the ancestor of the messiah.

She agreed to speak to him after the weekend with one caveat. I had to pretend I did not know he was a *ger*, as she had broken her word to him by telling me. He didn't want people to know, and he'd be very upset with her if he knew she told me. *Oy.* Okay. Deal.

Ger did like me, but he told her that he didn't want to date me, because he was sure that if I knew the truth, I would turn him down. Except that I *did* know the truth and I would not turn him down. Except we couldn't tell him that. This was complicated.

She prevailed on him and tried to tell him that it didn't matter. Nope, he wouldn't hear of it. She finally admitted to him that she had told me. He was sore at her betrayal, but astonished that I had agreed. It took a while, but he eventually took my number.

He didn't call.

A couple of weeks later, my phone rang, but when I answered it, I heard a dial tone. That happened several times. *Hmm.* One evening, he finally did call, but a moment or two after our hellos we seemed to disconnect, and he did not call back. I didn't have his number and caller ID was not yet widespread. *Why didn't he just call back? Did he think I had hung up on him? Had he hung up on me?* I had no idea what was going on. I was beginning to wonder if he was paranoid or crazy.

The next evening, he called again. We lived far from each other, so decided to meet in the city after work. We made up a time to meet, but he said he would call me in the office when he was close to the city. He was an hour late, and still hadn't called. I knew it would be a long wait. I was ready to go home, but remembering the Torah mandate to be kind to a convert, I waited. He arrived over two hours late. I was very hungry, but he did not offer any explanation nor apologize, and took me out for drinks. Didn't he realize that it was way past dinnertime and I had waited over two hours for him?

Ger told me about his journey to Judaism which I found fascinating. He admitted that I was the only *frum*-from-birth woman who ever knowingly dated him. He told me all the rabbis were eager to teach him about Judaism, but then when he wanted a date, they all said, "not my daughter!" If it was truly because he was a convert, that is very sad. But perhaps their refusals had nothing to do with his conversion. During the course of the conversation, I learned he had no viable means of supporting a family. He had called and hung up numerous times, seemed paranoid, and had been over two hours late. I didn't want another date, but it was not because he was a convert.

I went home and I cried. I cried because I went to too many *Shabbatonim*; I cried because I slept on the floor; I cried because the cookies had ants; I cried because the hostess berated me; I cried because I waited weeks for this date; I cried because converts can't get dates; I cried because I waited over two hours for Ger; I cried because I'd never wait that long for a man again; I cried because I knew I'd be chastised for not waiting. I cried for all of those reasons and more. I cried to God and begged Him to end all this pain and humiliation because I could not take much more of it.

A few weeks later, I opened the *Jewish Press* and saw a display ad from a yeshiva wishing their alumni a *mazel tov* upon his engagement to So-and-So's daughter – the very daughter who had been home the week I slept on the family's floor! A yeshiva doesn't take out ads for just anybody – clearly this guy was wealthy or scholarly, or both. I cried because I knew I had been right – that when it came to their kids' marriage partners, status and wealth counted more to some people than anything else.

Crying Shame

I had a second date. Our first had been at a museum, and I hoped this time, we'd get to know each other better and truly break the ice. Things looked promising, and I would give it my best shot. He treated me to dinner at a nice restaurant and started chatting. He mentioned his cousin. He was very close to her and she had recently gotten married. *And she this... And she that... and her husband this.... and her husband that...* dots were being connected in my mind. *Could it be?* I finally asked, "What's your cousin's name?" He told me and I realized his cousin... was "Mrs.YeshivaGuy." My mind was startled by this revelation – *YeshivaGuy was married to this man's cousin!* I was not going to get into it with him.

Oblivious to the shock and turmoil in my mind, he chatted some more. *Why am I surprised he's married? He was a good catch for some yeshiva girl. Of course, men have it easier. But why would God allow a guy who had hurt me so much to find someone before I did?* My mind was in a resentful whirl and something in me broke the dam. My tears pushed through. I excused myself and went to the bathroom where I cried and then tried to compose myself. I looked at myself in the mirror. My makeup had smeared; my eyes were red. I took several deep breaths, wiped my face and then went back out to him. Cousin was a nice guy and didn't deserve this.

"Are you okay? I don't know what's going on. The last several girls I've dated have burst into tears in the middle of the date. Did I do something wrong?"

"Not at all." In fact, I was sure, I had just done something wrong. I had ruined this date. But then again, did I really want to have YeshivaGuy as a cousin?

"Did my cousin ever do something to you?"

"Um... no. of course not. I just thought of something sad and I couldn't hold the tears in. I'm really sorry."

We pushed through the rest of our dinner. He was a perfect gentleman, but I was a mess. I knew this wouldn't work out.

A few weeks later the phone rang and I picked it up to hear a voice I had not heard in ages. It was YeshivaGuy.

"Hi," he said. It had been years. His familiar voice evoked difficult memories and emotions.

I didn't know what to say. I was numb. I was angry. He was married and had been cruel to me. *Let him say whatever he has to say*. I had nothing to say.

"My wife's cousin told me about his date. He didn't mention your name but he said enough stuff for me to figure out it could be you."

I didn't want to talk.

"Well, if just hearing about me can do that to you, I must've been really mean to you."

"...Yes," my throat was scratchy. I was frozen. I had spent so much time confiding in and sharing and dreaming about this man. I had spent a year crossing off dates on a calendar for this man. He had spoken about marrying me. He had met someone on the plane. He had slammed the car door shut. He had turned me off from yeshiva guys. The pain was engulfing me afresh.

"I'm sorry. I never meant to hurt you."

"Yes, you did. You slammed the car door. On purpose."

"I'm so embarrassed. I was young and stupid. I wish I could undo that."

I didn't know what his apology was worth because, in the end, he was married and I was not. I had shattered and never recovered all the broken pieces. This call was making me relive my humiliation and experience its sharp edges all over again. My thoughts were racing as he talked.

He said if I was ever in the area, I should come for a meal. *That would be awkward.* And how he wished I was married. *Really? Except not to you.* That I was a special person. *Which is why you didn't call me when you returned.* That I deserved the best.

He was trying. But it was too little, too late. He wanted a clear conscience. He felt guilty and this call was for him. Could he really undo the damage? The alienation I felt from yeshiva guys? The reason I responded to Jr.Engineer's kindness? The guilt I felt for everything that followed. Could he piece together all the tiny shards of my heart? *Could he ever fix that?* I was working hard to fix that. He couldn't fix what he didn't even know he'd damaged. How could he know the long-term effects of what his actions had done to me? He didn't. It was only after Cousin's story that he understood that there *were* long-term effects. I intensely disliked this man and everything he stood for. I felt he cared more about his conscience than about me. What did I want from him? What more could I expect him to do? I didn't know. He wasn't the same person anymore. He had grown. He had found the courage to call me. He was trying to make amends. He was a better person now. I would be gracious and accept his apology. I must try to be a better person too.

Dear God, help me to continue searching. Help me to stay strong. And please, please, please, in the merit of my parents, my good deeds, my ability to forgive, please forgive my sins and please bring my husband to me.

Another string of dates brought me no closer to the *chuppah.*

There was a handsome man who was painfully shy.

There was the librarian who sounded great on paper but was a bundle of nervous awkwardness in real life.

There was the guy who took me to a crowded, dirty pizza shop full of kids on a Saturday night. It was not the right venue or atmosphere for a first date.

There was a guy who was very feminine – his movements, his voice, his laugh. I could tell he was trying to hide the fact that he was gay. Was he in denial? Trying to change? Was I reading too much into his mannerisms? I sometimes got the uncomfortable feeling people assumed I was gay because I was still single, and I knew they were very wrong. So, was I misjudging him? Everything about him turned my gaydar on. He seemed off in every way. I felt pain for anyone in that predicament. As bad as things were for me, I had more hope than he ever would. I felt aggrieved on his behalf.

It was painful to see him fight to do the right thing, but would he ever be happy? Once, I had asked a teacher in school why God would create people with this urge and then label it sinful, her reply was, "Why ask? Are you gay?" She hadn't taken my question seriously. Instead, she cast aspersions on me, while I was trying to make sense of the senseless. As an older adult, I posed this question to a rabbi, and while not totally satisfactory, he told me that everyone had challenges and tests in life.

"But rabbi, in this respect, you've been happily married since a young age. You can't know the struggle of an Orthodox gay man."

"No," he said, "but married men still have to overcome temptation and their desire for multiple women."

"*Oh…*" As a woman, that did not seem like such a difficult challenge to me, especially as this rabbi's wife was a beautiful woman. But a man's nature is very different from a woman's. Had he just obliquely admitted to me that he struggled with this? Perhaps. But at the end of the day, he still had a beautiful spouse and family without living a lie.

Seed of Friendship

I often had great conversations with men on the phone, only to meet and see the dynamics change entirely. This watershed date turned out to be the complete reverse.

I was set up by a professor. He had matched up students and had gained a reputation as a kind and caring matchmaker, so others contacted him as well. He gave my number to a gentleman who sounded like the kind of person I would want to meet. I was looking forward to the call, but when it came, I was disappointed. The conversation was stilted and the guy just sounded off. I did not want to go out with him, but this was truly a labor of love for the professor. He had been so kind to me and had spent time getting to know me. I didn't have the heart to cancel his suggestion. Too often, I felt obliged to follow through for the matchmaker's sake more than my own, even when I was certain I was not the slightest bit interested.

I was not looking forward to this date. He picked me up and he seemed very nervous and uncomfortable in his own skin. His green eyes disconcerted me a bit. My phone assessment was right. He was Singular. We went to a restaurant and I saw a married former classmate of mine two tables over which made this twice as intolerable. Spending time with an undesirable date feels as stifling as being momentarily stuck in an elevator with a scary person. I wanted to escape – a feeling I encountered far too often on dates. But I had survived in the past and would survive this too.

Like a child covering his eyes in a game of peekaboo and thinking no one else can see him, I pretended not to see my classmate. I focused on my date and tried to make conversation. *Then something changed.* He started being a little less nervous and a little more interesting. To my surprise, I found myself drawn by what he had to say. This was a first – having a bad phone call turn into a decent date.

Our second date started off similar to the first. *Oh my God, why did I agree to a second date with this guy?* But then, once more, the conversation flowed till I didn't notice Singular's flaws. On the drive home, I mentioned that I skated Sunday mornings in a nearby playground that had a hockey rink. I'd go early before the leagues showed up to get a bit of exercise. In fact, it was just down the street from where we were, so he said, "Is that so? Let's check it out," and he sharply turned the steering wheel, careening down the street. We got out of the car and went into the playground. The rink was dark and deserted. No one was there any longer and there were just a few people in the playground sitting at the chess tables. I imagined us two skating alone in the dark, but we didn't have skates with us.

"Would you like to go on the swings?" he asked.

"I'd love to," I said, pleased that he had asked. He took off his jacket and tie. We sat on the swings side by side and I tugged on my knee-length skirt so it wouldn't ride up. Singular's long legs swung him higher and faster. I pumped my legs hard to catch up and go as high. The air felt cool and fresh. My skirt and hair flapped back and forth with the wind of our movements. I was glad to see his spirited side, that he didn't worry about any rule book saying this was not proper etiquette on a second date. He was being himself, and I liked that a lot.

We both leaned back to enjoy this child-like wonder, stretched our legs out and stared silently at the stars while our airborne swings gradually wound down to gentle hypnotic waves. Looking heavenward, the peace of the evening blanketed us. We could forget we were in a garbage-strewn concrete playground in Brooklyn. We could forget we were on a date. In that shared moment, both of us were miles away from reality, and a seed of friendship, as tiny as the stars above us, had been sown. I wanted to stay there for hours, but when we looked earthward again, the park was creepy, deserted, littered concrete. Nothing like the soft velvet of the soaring skies we had shared. We returned to the car, but something had changed between us. We would have another date.

We went out several more times, and each time I'd feel as though it was our first meeting. Something was not quite right, but I didn't know what. *Were we not right for each other? Were we afraid?* Perhaps looking back, we could've been helped with coaching or guidance, but neither of us thought of that and we mutually agreed to move on.

I pressed on.

There was the man who didn't drive and asked me to meet him at a restaurant in Brooklyn. He arrived 45 minutes late and subsequently told me he lived right around the corner.

There was the first cell phone guy. We chose to meet on a street corner in the city after work. I waited, wondering how late this fellow would be and why I'd agreed to wait for him in the street. Suddenly behind me I heard a one-sided disembodied conversation. There was no phone booth nearby. I turned around. A guy with a *kippah* motioned with his hands and his lips, asking me if I was his date, and if I could wait while he held a phone to his ear. Let's just say my first interaction with him and with cellphones was not a good one.

I needed to do something drastic.

Drastic Measures

I had gone to so many *shuls* and so many singles' events in so many neighborhoods. And I had tried every matchmaker in town. *God, I know it's only You I can depend on. Help me out here.* I prayed and prayed and increased my volunteering and good deeds, but nothing helped. *Okay, let's go drastic another way.*

I needed to expand my horizons and find new avenues to meet men. I went to a local singles' lecture given by a rabbi who was a family friend. This was not a very popular event, and in fact, when I showed up there was just a handful of older men.

The synagogue, however, was built in a charming Egyptian/ Moorish architectural style and the rabbi was a great speaker – which sparked an idea. *This would be a great venue for an event!* I could drum up people through word of mouth. I could help others, and perhaps meet someone new myself.

I spoke to the rabbi, and before I had even elaborated on my idea, this caring man agreed and said he would not charge us for use of the synagogue. I thought we could do a Saturday night *Melave Malka* around Chanukah time. The rabbi could speak as well as give an architectural tour of this historic synagogue. I recruited some friends to help plan and publicize this event.

We would charge only five dollars, to recoup our expenses and buy the rabbi a gift. I was not looking to profit off singles, and I knew too well how exploited I felt when I paid for an event only to find nothing planned and little food. At one gathering organized by a "reputable" *shadchan*, the only thing served – to everyone's dismay – was sliced celery on paper plates. There was nothing else, not even dips or dressing! *Had something gone wrong with her food order or was this planned?* There was no program at all, just a room for mingling. It felt as though they didn't consider us worth the effort.

While there are many sincere people and matchmakers willing to help singles, as this rabbi was willing to, there were matchmakers who made little effort to acquaint themselves with singles, suggest any dates, nor follow up when called with inquiries about people. Too many people who billed themselves as *shadchanim*, were not. They were perhaps seeking accolades, *shidduchim* for their own kids, a hobby, a social group or a new income stream. Others seemed to be for-profit event planners. My friends and I would be the not-for-profit event planners.

We planned to have snacks, pastries, and drinks and bought decorative platters and cutlery to dress up the tables. We would have a program, a speech, a tour, and mingling.

Shortly before the event, we discovered someone had decided to plan a last-minute *Shabbaton* the same weekend as our event. That would cut the number of attendees down. On Friday the weather forecast threatened a snowstorm. I expected a complete and utter disaster. *God, if you will not help me, why won't You allow me to help others?*

Yet, the night of the event, people did show up. Not as many as I had planned for, but a nice amount. The rabbi scanned the room and asked, "Where did you get all these people from?"

He was amazed at how my friends and I had gotten these people by word of mouth only. They had come out in the snow. I don't know whether any couple met at that event and married. My hope was that people had networked, and perhaps somewhere down the line, it helped someone somehow. It was a modest success.

I prayed to God. *I did my part and put in my effort to help others, could You please help as well?* We had recouped our expenses and had just enough extra to buy the rabbi a beautiful silver *mezuzah*.

Touchy Subject

I found a roommate through a mutual friend and we started looking for an apartment. My European parents were not thrilled, but my mother understood how I felt. I was getting older and girls who had gotten married at nineteen had more independence than I did. I had wanted to move out years before, and knew American kids who had done so, but for my European father this was incomprehensible. "She doesn't want to get married!" he exclaimed to my mother.

He probably worried about what I'd be getting into, not realizing I'd already had done things he disapproved of while living right under his roof. His fears were unfounded because I still was deeply connected to God and still very much wanted to get married. But time was marching on. I was an adult and the move was way overdue. Additionally, there is a Jewish belief that if one changes one's place, one can change one's *mazel,* and I desperately needed a change of *mazel.* My roommate and I started our search.

A few months later, I ran into Swell. I had seen him around in the past, but he always seemed to be dating someone or other. Swell reminded me a bit of Look. He had lots of girlfriends, was smooth and suave. I had learned my lesson and was sure I didn't want to go down that road again. But I did not want to pre-judge him. If I could give all the socially awkward men a chance, it would be a relief to give someone like him a chance too.

I was looking forward to getting to know him better. He took me out for ice cream. We had fun choosing toppings and found a corner table. I felt so thrilled to have a comfortable date. Then on the car ride home, in the middle of nowhere, he casually asked me, "Are you *shomer negiah?*" This means "Do you observe the 'laws of touch'?" or in plain English, "Do you kiss and make out, or is that out of bounds?" I found the question inappropriate and very undignified. My heart sank.

"Why do you ask?" I said, though I knew *exactly* why someone would ask. "Are you only open to dating me if you can touch me?"

"Oh no, no, no, no… of course not," he backtracked. I suppose he either liked me enough to date me without touching me or he was up for the challenge of changing my mind.

I was disappointed that he had asked. And I must confess that at that moment I didn't know the answer to his question. In general, I was a sincere, religious girl praying to God to allow me to meet my mate the kosher way. I did not want to engage in taboo behaviors, though I knew that others did. On the other hand, I was young and had a normal libido which I was forced to suppress. I had slipped up on occasions and fallen beneath my own standards.

It seemed crude to me that he had asked. For people who do touch, the moments arise naturally. *They don't ask.* Other than that *faux pas,* the date went well so I didn't want to be too quick to dismiss him.

We continued to date and during that time, I finally moved in with my roommate. Swell helped me with my first big supermarket expedition to stock my fridge and pantry. It felt so nice to have someone to share my mundane tasks with, and it was my first continuous relationship in some time. And it happened when I had moved. I felt hopeful that perhaps moving had indeed changed my *mazel.* Maybe things would work out this time.

Swell always came up with original ways to spend time together that weren't costly, so I wasn't turned off as I was by cheap men. He was kind to my roommate too. He'd come up and chat with her for a bit, before taking me out. I found it considerate and endearing that he didn't just ignore her, pick me up, and whisk me away. I was growing very fond of him and things seemed to be progressing.

One day he inched toward me and tried to kiss me and I only had a moment to decide what to do. I rationalized that we had been dating a while now, and I could see myself marrying him. I was attracted to him and I thought perhaps this was the way other women lock down their grooms. Perhaps my refusals had been my mistake all along. *This time he didn't ask.* I wanted someone sincere about Judaism which Swell seemed to be, but I wanted someone who straddled both the Jewish world and the modern world too. He seemed to fit the bill. Perhaps I should relax my standards and join the club. With him, I could forgive myself for the lines I had crossed in the past. But I did feel guilty on several fronts. This was a betrayal of God and certainly a betrayal of my father's expectations. Wasn't this behavior *exactly* what my father feared? I had barely moved out and it had already happened.

Swell called me for a date, and when he showed up, he said, "Can we sit for a few minutes? There's something I want to talk to you about."

"Sure! Come in. Can I get you some water?"

"No, no, I'm fine." He seemed a bit nervous. "You know things are going really swell between us and, you know, you and I really get along." *Yes, I thought so too.* I was a bit startled. *Was he...? Could it be...?* I dreamed of getting engaged but could this really be happening? This was unexpected, but surely welcome.

He continued, "You know, the next logical step would be to get engaged..." My head was spinning. It was happening. "But I'm not ready, so I think we have to break up."

Like a roller coaster that slowly climbed a hill and then sped down the other side, I crashed. I was shocked. *He was breaking up with me? Because things were going too well?* This came out of nowhere. I had even let him touch me.

Then the clincher. "You're not religious enough for me," said the hypocrite who had pressured me to break my own religious convictions. I was more *machmir* than he was. *What was he talking about?* I was stunned speechless and let him say whatever he wanted to and just waited for him to leave. Then I went into my bedroom before my roommate came home – to bury myself in my blanket and cry out my pain, my shame, my anger. I was inconsolable.

The next morning, I resolved that I would not grieve or give this man another moment of my time. I had wasted a year scratching dates on a calendar for YeshivaGuy. I had wasted time mourning over Look. I had learned from my mistakes and this time I would not waste another minute. I would thank God for sparing me. I had survived the other breakups and would survive this one too. I would say *Gam zu l'tova. This too, is good.* And I would move on. Fast.

Roadblock

A friend called with a blind date suggestion. I truly wanted to drop out of the world for a while, but this time I was determined not to wallow in self-pity. I promised myself I would move on. So, I pushed myself to agree to the date. I was told he was younger than me, and I did not have a problem with that – Look had been younger – but I wondered why a younger man would agree to a blind date with an older woman. It had never happened. Look and I had met on our own. Was this man desperate? Was he unable to get dates? I was a bit nervous.

The man who showed up was surprisingly easy on the eyes, except that he wore a very strange pointy colorful *kippah* along with his formal suit. I wasn't embarrassed to be seen with him, but I was disconcerted by his *kippah*. He also seemed very nervous throughout our chat. I discovered most of what I had been told about him was inaccurate or incorrect, but we had a pleasant time. He seemed like a decent fellow and had a hint of a charming Texas accent. He hadn't grown up religious and now seemed to be unsure of where he belonged on the observance spectrum. That was fine with me. As I overlapped various segments of religious society, I was more comfortable with others who also didn't fit neatly into one niche. When I expressed my surprise that he had agreed to date an older woman when many men my age or older wrote me off, he said that he knew others that were happily married to older women. I attributed his willingness to open-mindedness.

Our mutual friend called to say that Accent was interested in a second date. For our second date he showed up in a nice shirt, slacks and a nice blue felt *kippah*. I was very relieved. "Oh, I'm so glad you're not wearing that odd *kippah* you wore last time."

He smiled. "Bought it specifically for our date. I was told you were artsy, and thought it'd be cool and impress you more. But I heard you didn't like it."

"No! You wore that to impress me?"

"Yes," he laughed. "Guess I was wrong on that score."

"You were! I used to do that too – dress a certain way anticipating what my date would prefer. But in the end, I think we just have to be ourselves and find someone who likes us for who we are. I definitely like your ordinary *kippah* better." We laughed over it. I was glad I had waded right back into dating. He was easy to talk to. Perhaps God had rewarded me for doing the right thing? Perhaps moving to my new apartment had truly changed my luck?

We continued to date, and over time two things happened. My feelings for him grew, but my concern over whether I could marry him or not, grew as well.

I liked him and he seemed to like me back. Conversations flowed and we had an easy rapport. I truly felt I could be myself. Nothing he said made me feel on guard or uncomfortable.

We were interested in each other, but there were major issues. He didn't have the job I was told he had. That was one problem. One couldn't support a family on his salary at all. We talked about it and he told me how his parents had divorced. His father moved far away and his mother had remarried more than once. He had not had a stable family life or support system. I thought perhaps we could work something out if he went back to school. I would gladly support him through it. I was willing to do what it takes. Now I understood why he was open-minded about age.

I wanted it to work, but deep down inside, I did not relish the thought of being the second sibling marrying ahead of my sister. I talked to her about it, and to her credit, she assured me that if I felt it was right, I should go ahead. I invited her along on one of our dates, because I wanted to include her and felt terrible about possibly marrying ahead of her. It weighed on me despite her assurances.

My roommate found Accent a bit reserved compared to Swell, but thought well of him too. She suggested I take genetic tests to rule out any chances that we were both carriers of the same genetic diseases common to Ashkenazic Jews because of in-breeding. This is common practice for young adults who take these tests before ever getting set up. As it had not been as common when I started dating, I had never done it. I did it now because I felt Accent was a serious contender. He took the test as well. He too had not done it before. We were relieved to discover we didn't share any defective genes. This test made it all feel real, despite my concerns.

In the midst of this, Swell called. He had heard through the grapevine that I had a new "boyfriend." I didn't consider Accent a boyfriend, I considered him a potential husband. I didn't appreciate Swell's questions. He grilled me and wanted to know how we had met and who this guy was. As *he* had broken up with *me*, I didn't feel the need to share any information and refused to talk about it. Swell was bitter, as though *I* had dumped *him*. He said things to deliberately hurt me. "Are you sure you're religious enough for him? You sure weren't for me." This mean streak and swollen ego had not appeared till he broke up with me. It made me question my judgment; suddenly I feared marrying a mistake.

I suspected that he was hoping for the drama and tears that usually followed a break-up, but I had surprised him by appearing to take it well (though I hadn't) and moving on so quickly. He sounded possessive, even jealous. In response to his taunts, I reflected that I was religious enough for Accent. We had discussed both of our religious journeys, the mistakes we had made in the past, and the future we both wanted. All was good on that front.

However, on the other front, nothing was resolved. I was willing to help him through school and even finance it if I had to, but he couldn't or wouldn't come up with a plan. He was a bright guy and I was sure he could do it if he put his mind to it. But his mind was on marriage, not school or work. I didn't mind if he drove a jalopy, or we weren't rich. I didn't need to marry a doctor or a lawyer, but I didn't want to be the primary breadwinner. I wanted to feel love, friendship and respect for my partner. Two out of three wasn't enough. This man didn't have a solid way to support a family. It was hard to find time to date as his schedule varied and it would be even more challenging as a married couple.

My family was supportive of me and shared my concern, but were also open to helping him work it out. They wanted me married. Some people implied I was a Jap and should not worry about it. "Plenty of people have no money and are happily married, and besides, things will work out after marriage." But I didn't want to marry someone to land on welfare. While others told me that I deserved better, I didn't think that was the case. He hadn't had family support because of events beyond his control. *How do any of us know where we'd be in his shoes?* I didn't want to give up so easily.

One day at work the receptionist buzzed me to say I had a special visitor out front. I wasn't expecting anyone, so I was very surprised to see Accent waiting for me in the reception area. His face broke into a smile. I couldn't help laughing.

"What are you doing here? Aren't you supposed to be at work right now?"

"You told me you like surprises. We never had a lunch date, so thought I'd surprise you with one." He had biked over the bridge to meet me. He was my knight in shining armor.

"He's as cute as his accent," the receptionist whispered to me as I went back to get my purse. I loved the surprise and was touched that he had biked all this way for me when he should have been working. We walked over to Bryant Park and had our all-too-short lunch date before I had to return to the office. I waved him off, "Be careful!"

An hour later he called, "Hi, what's up?" I asked.

"I'm at the hospital."

"What? Were you hit?" I was always afraid of the way he zipped through city traffic.

"No. I started ridin' home, and next thing you know, I woke up in an ambulance." He had fallen asleep while riding because he was over-tired. Luckily, he had not been hit or run over. Thank God. But he didn't have health insurance. I knew that because we had that talk and he told me his job offered it, but he hadn't signed up because it was expensive. Now he would have to pay for the ambulance and hospital out of pocket.

I cared very much about him, but I was beginning to fear that this is what my life would be like. One disaster after another. I would be his caretaker and mother, not his partner and wife. I agonized over this and truly did not know what to do. My feelings for him had grown. We were so compatible religious-wise. We shared a great sense of humor. We cared about many of the same things. I enjoyed spending time with him, was attracted to him, even fell in love with him. But as much as I tried, I couldn't envision marrying him.

I was afraid I was at a fork in the road and I would not be able to retrace my steps. *Perhaps this was my last chance to have a child.* I recalled disturbing advice I had once received: "If you can't find someone, marry anyone, have a kid, then get divorced." I could not see myself doing something that could destroy three people's lives. It struck me as incredibly selfish. Even in this case, where I truly cared for Accent, I could not marry him with a backup plan to divorce him if things didn't work out. That would be cruel. I could not marry him only because I wanted a child. That would be the totally wrong reason to marry someone.

He had proposed, and I said, "Not yet." I had a clear, but difficult, choice here that could change my destiny. I could undo my "singleness" with a "yes."

I wanted to marry him, but not this way. Any talk we had about improving his situation went nowhere. I wanted to marry a responsible, grown-up man, not someone who stumbled through life. He wanted a family any which way because he'd never had a stable one. I wanted to marry him with the belief that my marriage would succeed, not with the fear that it wouldn't.

I finally broke up with him, though I didn't want to.

The start of summer is the worst possible time to break up with someone. The sun is shining, everybody is out. And in New York City, when one feels lonely, all one seems to see are couples strolling hand-in-hand.

This time it was far harder for me to push myself to move on, but I tried. I had a blind date in the city after work shortly afterwards. The man was nervous as anything. He accidentally tipped his plate over and the contents went flying. Tomato sauce splattered onto my blouse. The conversation was inane. Pieces of his food dribbled into his beard. I lost my appetite and despaired.

I wanted it to be over. After our date, I was doing all I could to fight the tears. I thought it best that I walk off my tears in Central Park rather than go directly into the subway to cry in full view of other passengers. I felt pathetic. *God, is this my fate? Just one bad date after another? What would happen to me? I could suffer through this if I had a crystal ball and knew it would all end well. But if my fate is never to marry, please God spare me further indignity. I have had my fill, God. I have.*

I second-guessed myself. Had I been wrong to break off with Accent? I walked deeper into the park as the sun was sinking beyond the horizon, and discovered that it was the premiere night for the "Shakespeare in the Park" performance. Usually, the lines for free tickets are impossibly long, but as this was the first night of the season, there were a few single seats available and the show was about to start. Would I want a free ticket? a gentleman asked. On the spur of the moment, I took the ticket. The play was great and the summer night was perfect, but my heart was heavy. On each side of me were happy couples who had gone out for a pleasant evening. I was alone with my self-pity, in a tomato-sauce-splattered blouse – sitting in the outdoor theater silhouetted by dark trees and covered by a starlit sky. I felt sorrier for myself than ever. *Why did I fail at all my relationships? Why did the men I cared for, like me, but not enough to marry me? Why did the one man who did want to marry me, not have his act together?* On this night, my self-esteem plummeted.

Between my tearful prayers to God, I pushed myself some more. I went to a singles' barbecue at Riverside Park and everyone there seemed so wrong for me. Too old, too awkward. I had just broken up with a handsome, fit, younger man who I enjoyed talking to. Sigh. *Was I shallow? Would any of us ever find our matches?* This summer would be torturous.

Singular Events

I had friends who went to *Shabbatonim* sponsored by the same groups over and over again, and the same people would show up time after time. Then I'd hear the same complaints about there being no new people, so I tried to shake things up. I heard about a family *Shabbaton* in Crown Heights. It was not a weekend designed to introduce singles to each other, but rather to introduce people and families to the Chabad lifestyle. I had gone to a Chabad summer camp years ago, so that wasn't the draw for me. The reasons that drew me to this *Shabbaton* were twofold. Chabad worked hard at bringing Jews back to their roots and many became religious – not necessarily Lubavitch – so perhaps I could meet a suitable gentleman. At the least, I could network with a different crowd – people who may know available men. Also, my parents had lived in Crown Heights as newlyweds. I had visited several times for weddings, but it would be nice to experience the neighborhood and explore – maybe check out the building I had once lived in as an infant.

I asked friends if they would like to join me, but none were interested. Determined to expand my horizons, and forget about Accent, I signed up on my own. When I showed up on Friday to sign in and find out whose home I'd be sleeping at, there was a line. Then I spotted the back of someone's head. *Could it be him?* There was a single man on the line who I recognized and was happy to see. It was Singular!

"Hi, Singular!" He twirled around.

"What are you doing here?" he smiled broadly.

"I guess the same thing you are," I smiled back. *What a coincidence, I thought, or was it? Weird.*

"I'm glad to see a face I know. This should be interesting," he said.

"Yes," I scanned the crowd, "it looks like most people are married or older, not too many singles here."

Without the pressure of a formal date, we had an amazing weekend. We spent all our meals together chatting. We were clearly on the same wavelength, open to meeting new people of differing observance levels, willing to take chances without friends joining us.

Maybe I should pay attention to Singular. Maybe God wanted me to notice him. If only he felt the same way. Where I saw Divine Providence, Singular only saw coincidence.

Weeks later, a matchmaker called me and told me she had found the "perfect" guy for me. So many others had used that word, I didn't feel very enthusiastic. But then she told me the guy's name – it was Singular! By this time, I was convinced that perhaps Singular *could* be the perfect guy. Well – not a perfect person, but the perfect person for me. But we had tried a second round of dating and had discussed it. Singular was convinced that I was not his *basherte*.

"I would go out with him and I agree he's perfect for me, but he's convinced that I'm not the person for him."

"What if I talk to him?"

"Sure. Good luck with that and let me know," I said, hoping she'd changed his mind. But she called me with her regrets that he had not.

A few days later, my brother was having surgery in Manhattan. I had a job interview scheduled nearby, and I hoped to visit him afterwards. But I was lugging my heavy portfolio. It occurred to me that I could call Singular, who worked in the area, ask him if I could drop off my portfolio and then continue on without all that weight. All the awkwardness between us was long gone and I knew where he stood regarding "us," so it really was just a matter of dropping off my portfolio after the interview and picking it up before he left for the day. Singular said it was okay, but when I showed up, it seemed more than okay. He appeared to be thrilled to see me though just days ago, he told the matchmaker we were not a match. I was confused, as always. He clearly liked me. *Perhaps marriage scared him?* I did not know, but I thought it best not to broach the subject.

I spent the afternoon running around doing several errands in my interview heels, and then I walked all the way to the hospital to see my brother. I was told he was still in surgery. *Why had I not thought to bring along flats?* My feet were pinched and raw by then. I quickly limped to Singular's office to retrieve my portfolio and hoped I'd get a seat during the rush hour subway ride home.

"Thanks so much! It made things much easier for me," I reached out for it.

Singular turned his torso, and held my portfolio away from me playfully. "I can't let you go home when you've been running around all afternoon. You must be starving! Let me take you out for dinner," said the guy who had just told the matchmaker *a few days ago* that he didn't want to go out with me.

I was elated (and confused) that he wanted to treat me to dinner, but I was exhausted and my toes were on fire much more than my heart at this moment. "Thanks so much, that's really sweet, but I'm just too tired. I really just need to go home."

"I insist," he said, and with that he strode out of the building expecting me to follow. He stayed well ahead of me to keep my portfolio out of reach and I was too tired to think. I didn't know whether I was upset or glad, but this man was torturing me. Singular turned around and saw that I was trailing far behind, gingerly taking small steps to minimize the blistering pain. "All the more reason to take you to dinner. You're gonna feel a whole lot better when you sit and have a meal, than standing in a rush hour subway. It's just one more block." I was in agony by then. We got to the restaurant and it was closed. Out of business!

"I can't believe this!" he said. "I was just here for lunch the other day!"

"That's obviously a sign from God, I should just go home," I winced in pain.

"No. no. God wants you to have a meal. Come this way. Just a few blocks," he smiled. *A few blocks? I could barely manage a few steps.* The man was distressing me, even though he thought he was helping. We finally got to the restaurant and it was dark and empty before dinner time.

He waved the manager over and introduced him to me, "This is my buddy. I come here all the time. He knows me." Then to the manager he announced, "This. Is. My. Friend."

They gave each other a knowing look. *Now what was that all about?*

Perhaps I did have a chance after all? I would have to rethink this clearly when my feet weren't occupying my thoughts.

We had a great meal, great conversation, and after dinner, he carried all my things for me as we made our way to the subway station. I was totally confounded by this man. When I broached the subject of dating again a few days later, he said, "You're not my *basherte*," with the same conviction as he had in the past. *Why had he been so thrilled to see me and treat me to dinner?*

Men are like a pair of high-heeled shoes. They could make women feel beautiful and pained at the same time.

Forever and a Week

I had survived the long, hot summer. Rosh Hashanah was coming up. Another year had passed and I was still single. I felt it acutely at this time of year, when God would judge who would live and who would die. Would He decide who would find a mate and who would not? It sometimes seemed like the world moved on, but I was running, forever running, and getting absolutely nowhere.

One morning, my doorbell rang. I ran to open the door and saw a red-ribboned package lying at my feet. My heart quickened and I picked it up. It was a box of chocolates from Accent with a sweet Rosh Hashanah card, wishing me well. He was probably hoping to reignite a spark or get another chance. I knew I had given it my all to make it work, and it had not. It would never work – and yet, this box melted my resolve. I called to thank him. It led to a reunion and the same conversations, struggles, talks that went nowhere. I could've easily gone back to having companionship and attention that I sorely craved, but that would've been selfish of me. I had to stop it now. I broke it off after another month of trying.

A short while later, he called me up and said, "Are you 100% sure? Would you get upset if I met someone else? Would you regret not marrying me?" *Hmm, has he met someone?* "Because I've met a nice girl, and if you won't marry me, I'll ask her." *What?*

"When did you meet her? We just broke up!"

"Just last week. But if it's not you, it's going to be her." *Last week? Oh. My. God. Chassidim do this with family vetting. But he was a guy rebounding from a broken heart. This is the sort of reckless behavior that scared me away from marrying him in the first place!*

"Are you for real? That's crazy! You told me you wanted to marry me!"

"I do. But I'm going to marry her if you won't marry me." As though we were easily interchangeable. We had spent a few months getting to know each other and he had seen her just three times. I thought of this woman, whoever she was, and how she would feel knowing her *chosson*-to-be was having this talk with someone else. I hoped he would grow to love her. I felt sorry about it all and this talk made me uneasy. I felt guilty. I was curious about her and he confided in me. He told me about her without telling her about me. Yet I was certain that I could not marry this man.

He proposed to her and I fell ill.

I stayed home from work, feeling depressed, disgusted, and discouraged. I begged God to give me clarity and to forgive me for my sins. The doorbell rang. The new *chosson* was standing there, holding a plate of toast. *What is he doing here? I don't know what to feel or do, God.* "I heard you were sick," he said. No one had told him, but he knew me well enough by then to know how I'd feel.

He was still very attached to me. Still willing to break off his engagement if I said yes. *What? You can't do things like that!* My emotions were flip-flopping from missing him to being absolutely horrified. His emotions were clearly unsettled too. I was there, but felt disembodied, as though watching the scene from above.

I was inexorably drawn in as a spectator fascinated by a crash scene. We stumbled through an awkward conversation and an awkward goodbye. I wished him well and knew I would miss him. But I closed that door. For good.

For his good. For her good. For my good. Forever.

Flowers from the Same Garden

The only upside to breaking up with someone I had hoped to marry was the relief I felt that I did not hurt my sister by marrying ahead of her. True, she had given me her blessing, but it would probably have felt devastating for her and diminished my happiness.

The tide soon turned and now she was seeing someone, and boy, was I rooting for her. I wanted this to work out for her more than anything, and miraculously it did. She got engaged. We were all jubilant, and once again I felt I had hit the jackpot, even though someone else was the bride. It was hard to feel happy every time another nineteen-year-old got married, but my sister was my sister and she was an older bride, so my joy was pure. We had both been dating so long that the fact she actually got engaged felt surreal. My brother remarked how his own wedding had been a *simcha*, but this one was a miracle. All of us felt the wonder of it.

I also felt strongly, perhaps now the ball would start rolling. It did, but not for me. My roommate got engaged shortly after that. Again, I felt so happy for her. I had watched her give her all to her husband-hunt and it had finally paid off. We had gone through years of disappointment, so it was great to share in the elation.

They say that sisters are different flowers from the same garden. If I am a rose, my sister is a peony – very much like a rose, but fluffier, all beauty and softness, no thorns. I was the one with the sharp thorns protecting my sensitivity. I would have to learn to soften. Our journeys were different, but we had indeed come from the same garden.

Boys and Girls

It doesn't matter how old you are, if you've never been married in the observant world, you are considered a "boy" or a "girl." If you are male, you are called up to the Torah in the synagogue as a *bachur* – a lad. The indignity of it should spur the bachelors to marriage. The older I grew, the less I wanted to date a *bachur*. I felt that one who had the companionship of a spouse or the responsibility of children, often had a certain gravitas that others who have never been married, including myself, do not. I myself was considered a "girl" but wanted to marry a "man," not a "boy."

I had responsibilities at work, obligations towards my parents and family, volunteered as a Big Sister, and offered help to others in need, yet I felt myself living a more juvenile life than I should've been. I was self-centered in a way that a married person cannot be. I could leave my lights on or off, my windows open or shut, set the alarm for any hour, never wait for my turn to shower. Of course, many married people are just as selfish, often to the chagrin of their spouse and at the price of their marital harmony.

When my roommate was packing up her things before her wedding and her impending move, she pointed out that her other roommates had gotten married and left her behind. This was the first time she was leaving a roommate behind.

"There was another difference."

"What's that?" I asked.

"You were the only roommate that reached out and reconciled after every fight," she said. I felt relief. *Maybe I'm not half bad after all.* I had made overtures to her, even when I had felt 100 percent certain that I was right and she wasn't, simply because it was in my own best interest to do so. Who wants to live with silence and anger? Who wants to hide in her room and avoid her roommate instead of having free reign of the whole apartment? I felt hopeful that it meant I was primed for marriage and compromise.

Within weeks of my roommate moving out, I was aware of how comfortable it is to be selfish and not consider another in one's daily routines. Living with a roommate is a far cry from living with a person to whom one is committed by marriage. A spouse is a person one is physically intimate with, answers to, shares a life and builds a home with. If you're angry with a roommate, you can choose to work it out or leave, but when one is angry with a spouse, the stakes are higher and leaving is more complicated.

As a "girl," circumstances at times made me feel out of place, stupid, or childlike: when I stood in line with men to sell my *chametz* and the rabbi disregarded me; when I attended a Tisha b'Av lecture and the speaker railed against singles for causing a "new holocaust;" when a salesman in a furniture store sailed right by me to assist a young couple who had entered the store after me; when I'd be the only single in a room full of married people or worse, as a friend related, she'd been shunted off to a children's table at a wedding. My self-esteem and that of other "girls" worked hard at combating all these pitiable moments.

I also held off on doing things thinking *I'll do that as soon as I marry*. My roommate had taken her microwave oven with her, and I had resisted replacing it for months thinking *my husband will have his own* or *we'll buy one together*. It was silly. In the same vein, the day I bought my apartment, I was in tears. Though it was fiscally wise, I had wanted to commit to a husband before committing to a mortgage. This was not the way I had imagined things happening. It took time to unpeel the layers of mental blocks preventing me from living fully.

As a single person, the expectation is that if you haven't married, you haven't had intercourse. I cannot speak for everyone, but I know that for myself, and for my peers, this was largely true. A teenage girl could be a married "woman," and though I was older, and perhaps wiser, I was still a "girl." A *besulah*. I wanted to be a woman.

Pushing Boundaries

In my despair at my continual failure, I decided I needed to push boundaries. I could not keep repeating the same tactics and expect to get different results. So, I opened myself up to people to the left of me religiously. Perhaps someone would be inspired to return to his religious roots – a *baal teshuvah*. I contacted a Conservative man online. I was honest about being Sabbath observant. Perhaps he needed a change too. He agreed to meet.

I realized that someone could spot me with this gentleman who did not wear a *kippah* nor fit the profile of whom I would usually date. They would have to wonder. I felt I needed to give myself a chance regardless of what people thought.

When we met for coffee, it immediately became clear to me that he didn't know what being a Sabbath observer entailed. Our talk was pleasant, he had normal social skills, and was employed – so he was a breath of fresh air. I spoke a bit about my background and religious practice and he seemed open to it. I grabbed onto that straw and we agreed to meet again. When he called and suggested meeting at a non-kosher restaurant on "Saturday," I was astonished that he still hadn't grasped my observance level. Or perhaps he did, and thought I was open to compromising my beliefs. I was willing to meet someone halfway, but no, I was not willing to desecrate the Sabbath or give up *kashrus*. I pointed out that I could not eat at a non-kosher establishment and that I could not meet on Saturday, and immediately sensed his disappointment. He finally understood that dating me would cramp his lifestyle. We never went out again and I felt foolish for having thought this tactic could work.

Stuck on Why

One of my activities was one-on-one study through Aish Hatorah. They paired me with an Irish convert, Colleen, whom I met weekly to study Jewish subjects. She told me that when her classmates had gone to France or Italy for their gap year, she chose to go to Israel instead. Colleen hadn't known any Jews and couldn't explain her desire to learn about Judaism except that she "always felt she was a Jew trapped in a non-Jew's body."

"Aha! Maybe I'm a non-Jew trapped in a Jew's body!" I exclaimed.

She laughed, "Only a Jew would come up with an idea like that!"

I was always heartened to hear the stories of *geirim* and *baalei teshuvah* and learn about the struggles on their journeys. The unnatural history of the Jewish people affirmed my belief in God. I didn't merely believe in Him. I knew Him. I felt Him. He was there. But when I felt crushed under the weight of humiliation or loneliness, or when life seemed unjust, I struggled. Jacob was called "Israel" which connotes "struggle," after struggling with the angel. We are *Bnai Yisrael*, the Children of Struggle. Hearing of the difficult paths and ultimate decisions of these people to be observant Jews helped me immensely. I wanted to be good and do good, and that's why I studied with Colleen weekly. It benefitted both of us.

We met in a large auditorium. Women paired with women learned on one side of the room. Men paired with men learned on the other side. Over time, I became friends with Colleen and introduced her to some of my friends. I invited her to a *Melave Malka* where the keynote speaker would be a former Irish priest. I thought she'd enjoy it, but after he spoke, she remarked that "he sounds so non-Jewish!" I thought so too, but it was funny to hear it from her. She loved the concept of a *Melave Malka* and she very much wanted to host one. She spoke to her rabbi about planning one in their community in the near future and I offered to help, as I had gone to many over the years.

One snowy evening during our learning session, I spotted Swell at the other end of the room. I was taken aback. Colleen asked me what was wrong and I told her I had recognized an ex.

She wanted me to point him out, so I did, and she exclaimed, "Oh, I know him!" Apparently, they had met a few years earlier. She went over to speak with him and he offered her a ride home. I didn't tell her how things had ended between us, so she asked him to take me as well. It was all very awkward, but he agreed. I didn't care, as it was snowy and I sat in the back seat where I wouldn't have to talk to him. In the car, she babbled easily, unaware of the underlying tensions between me and Swell. She mentioned the *Melave Malka* she was planning.

"When is this party? I could help out!" he offered. I was not thrilled, but it was not my business. *Let him help. He's her friend.*

That evening finally arrived. Colleen was giddy with excitement at the crowds filling her synagogue. Swell served as a waiter, which gave him the opportunity to flirt with all the women. I tried to focus on the *mitzvah* I had done by helping Colleen and enabling this event to happen. I would not let his presence spoil it.

I was standing with a group of women, when Swell held out a platter with a flourish and a witty remark. When he left, the woman standing next to me leaned over and asked, "Who is *that?*"

She was clearly enamored of him. I didn't want to say what I really thought of the guy who had asked me whether I was *shomer negiah*, dumped me for "not being religious enough," and then gotten jealous when I met someone else. "Oh, just some old friend," I answered. Her eyes followed him around the room. She was Smitten. I was sick to my stomach.

A few short hours later, Smitten was glued to Swell's side. They were touching each other in public. In a synagogue. In the presence of observant, lonely, single Jews. And especially in the presence of his ex, me, whom he had accused of not being religious enough for him. Now I was certain he was never the guy I was supposed to marry. He was all wrong for me. I would not behave that way. *Gam zu l'tova.* But it was difficult to watch.

A few months later, Smitten and Swell were engaged. *God, why did You DO this to me? Was it necessary for me to stand right next to her when she first laid eyes on him? Did I really need a front row view to their budding courtship? Did I have to do one-on-one learning with Colleen, help her plan a Melave Malka, or do the good deeds I did, to lead to this? To watch this hypocrite find HIS mate as a result of MY good deeds? Where is the justice? How do I recover from this? How do I continue to believe in You?*

I felt broken and angry. I felt the pain of decades of effort that had yielded no return. I thought of the biblical figure, Job, and the unendurable things he'd been through. God's answer had been "Are you God? Do you know My ways?" Maybe I was being punished for all my sins, for having hurt others. Maybe this would atone. But no. This felt like more than simple punishment. This felt like a cruel mockery of my good intentions.

I was not jealous of Smitten. Swell was not the man for me but I was angry at God and cut to the core. *How can You use my good deeds to slap me in the face like this?* Then I was mortified. How did I have the *chutzpah* to talk to God in that manner? Yet my mind kept reverting to my basic, agonizing question: Why would God reward that man and suffer me to witness it all unfold firsthand?

Why?

Why?

I was stuck on *Why.*

Forgiveness

A rabbi I had known for years called me with a suggested match. This was a rabbi I liked and respected, but I just didn't think he was good at matchmaking. Every suggestion he came up with for me seemed way off the mark. After dating so many men I understood some of my mistakes, whether it was wishing to date men who were out of my league or wasting time dating inappropriate men just to please matchmakers. I saw patterns in my dating. For instance, I always got along better with creative, philosophical men than with book-smart doctors or lawyers. I felt men who were out on their own or who had been married before were more mature than bachelors of advanced age still living with their parents. There were many other patterns and characteristics.

There could be exceptions to the patterns I was seeing. A doctor or lawyer could be creative too. A man could be admirable for staying home and caring for elderly parents. A bachelor could've just never met the right woman as so many women have never met the right man. But time and time again, the rule proved truer than the exception.

I was tired of dating and burnt out. I was losing my desire to date. Perhaps if I limited the unpleasant experiences as much as possible, I could retain a more positive view of the fewer dates I did go on. I no longer wanted to meet men just to please others or rack up the numbers because they say that "each date brings you one step closer to the right one." I wanted to date men who had realistic potential as my husband.

So, when this rabbi called with yet another older, never-married man who lived at home with his parents, I was not interested. The rabbi did not understand me.

"How can you know this man is not your match without meeting him? You can't know that!"

"You're right. I can't know that."

"Then try!"

"I'm not willing to take the risk on the off-chance that I'm wrong. My gut is telling me, based on all the men I've already met, that this guy won't be the one."

"That's the most ridiculous thing I've heard. Do you really want to get married? Believe me, I'm only calling you because I want you to get married!" he said as though he wanted me to get married *more* than I wanted me to get married.

He didn't lay awake nights wondering if his fate would be loneliness and childlessness. He didn't shed all the tears I'd shed. He didn't sit across the table in public from one man after another who couldn't string a few words into sentences. He didn't experience the rejection or humiliation I did for years on end. But he chastised me on and on. I had foolish ideas; I was being unreasonable; I was prejudiced and picky.

This was a rabbi I admired, but at this moment, I couldn't stand him. I knew he was married at a young age to the first woman he had met. She was a beautiful woman with the air of Grace Kelly about her. She was lovely in looks, temperament, personality, and character. When he finished his rebuke with, "Don't you see, I just want to help you?" the anger and pain welling up in me burst.

"Help me?" I burst out, "How is it *helping* me to lecture me for forty-five minutes and make me feel awful about myself? How?"

I couldn't believe I was speaking to him this way, but I could not hold back, "How old were you, Rabbi, when you got married? You do not know what it feels like to be in my shoes! You've never taken one step in the many miles I've walked. How old were you?"

He hesitated and clearly did not feel comfortable telling me.

"See? You can't even tell me how old you were when you got married? But I've had to tell matchmakers all my private information. I've done it again and again, and most of the time, it yielded nothing, not even a date. I've had to fill out forms, I've had to pay, I've had to reveal private information. I've had to be rejected over and over. I've had to reject others. I've had to run around to weekends and lectures and matchmakers and *Shabbatonim* and constantly put myself out there, and do all the things *you* haven't done even *once*. I've had to bear being lectured and told I was too picky, too old, too ugly, too this and too that for years now. I've been humiliated with questions about my fertility, suspicions that I was gay or abnormal in some way, constant inquiries about my age or looks, with no regard for my character or who I really am. Do you *really* think in all these years, I haven't already heard everything you've accused me of in the last forty-five minutes? Do you *really* think anything you've said helps? Because it doesn't. It doesn't help me at all. It just hurts!"

I stopped to catch my breath. My chest heaved. There was a silent pause. I was done.

The rabbi said nothing. Silence. It was thick. My veins were pulsing. I was trying to calm down. Had I really raged at him? Is this what I needed to do to keep from cracking? I had astonished myself. My fingers were twisting my hair nervously.

Then, softly, I heard, "I am so, so sorry. You are absolutely right. I had no idea. I hope you can forgive me."

I don't know what I was expecting to hear, but I was stunned to hear that. Over the years, none of the people who had lectured or shamed me had ever apologized for it. This was a first. Like Job's friends, when faced with the inexplicable, people often blamed the sufferer. It was human nature. Hearing the regret in his voice brought tears to my eyes. It took courage for the rabbi to say what he said. I admired him all over again. I felt so bad that I had ranted disrespectfully, and I apologized for that as well. But my rant had left us in a better place – understanding and forgiveness between us. I was grateful.

Conversion

Someone set me up with an Asian convert. I was open to that. I was more hesitant to learn that he was a black-hat yeshiva guy, the first one I would be going out with in a long time. YeshivaGuy had turned me off yeshiva guys way back, but converts were atypical so I agreed to see him. He was tall and handsome, wearing a suit and tie. When we entered the restaurant, people were throwing side glances at this Asian in a black hat. They were trying to be discreet about it, but I could feel their eyes on us. I was never comfortable drawing attention to myself on a blind date, even when the fellow was handsome.

GerTwo was personable, and unlike Ger who had told me he had been a devout Christian who turned to Judaism when the New Testament failed to answer his questions, GerTwo's story differed. He told me that while trying to learn English and reading American literature, he realized that all the writers he admired were Jewish, albeit secular. Out of curiosity, he began exploring Judaism, which started him on his path. He spoke with candor and humor and he was a perfect gentleman.

Whenever I meet a *baal teshuvah* or *ger* who overcomes so much – sometimes estranged from their families, struggling for acceptance in Jewish society, and studying everything from the language to the laws – it makes me wonder if I could do the same in their shoes. It makes me take stock of my relationship with God. I felt inadequate next to GerTwo. He was a very special person, and over the course of dinner, it became obvious to both of us that he was on a much higher spiritual plane than I was. While he discovered truth on his own through his explorations of Judaism, I was struggling. I believed in God, but recent events had me wrestling with the ultimate question of good versus evil and reward versus punishment.

The trials of being single were weighing me down. The fact that my prayers were unanswered, my *hishtadlus* unrewarded, pained me. The craving for companionship remained unsated. When a couple got engaged everyone claimed it was *basherte* – destined, but if I did not get engaged wasn't that *basherte* as well? Wasn't God in charge when things didn't go well, along with when they did? Why was I blamed for being picky? Was it my free will that left me alone? I didn't know what I believed, but the charming man across the table knew.

To my astonishment, he told me he yearned to be a Satmar Chassid. Satmar! That was not what I expected to hear, and it was not an option for me. We weren't at the same place and didn't share the same goals. There would be no conversion to Satmar for me. As much as I liked him, there didn't seem any point in continuing to see him. I wished him well and eventually learned that some lucky lady did marry him.

A Great Divorce

One day, a gentleman showed up with a beautiful bouquet of flowers on the first date. It was a nice gesture, but these flowers weren't for me. The *me* me. These were for whoever would greet him at the door. On our second date, he discussed marriage and whether I'd move to his city. While I was open to relocation, I did not know him or his city at all, so this question struck me as premature. *This is clearly a man on a mission.* He wasted no time in getting to know who I am or what my past was. He was trying to figure out the future.

He seemed to want a wife to replace his ex, who had been his high-school sweetheart. Yes, he said, they'd had a "great" marriage, a "great" relationship and got along "great", but he had returned to his Jewish roots and she was a non-Jew. *Ouch.* I felt sorry for this woman who didn't do anything wrong, who suddenly finds her life upended by this man's spiritual quest. He continued: his kids were "great," but he wanted "real" kids. *Ouch again.* Even as a religious woman who appreciated his desire to return to his roots, I wasn't crazy about the cavalier way he discounted his "great" kids and ex-wife. Where was the sorrow or regret for what he was putting them through? Or for the losses all around? I was turned off. I was on a different emotional wavelength.

A short while later, I thought of a woman I could set him up with. I called him to suggest it, and he told me he was already married. I hadn't foreseen that, but once he told me, I wasn't really very surprised. He was handsome and employed. He had a goal, a plan, and had moved at warp speed. *Mazel tov.*

More Singular Events

I was in a car with a gentleman on our way to lunch in the city. A friend had gone out with him and thought he'd be more suitable for me. During our initial phone call, he admitted that he had been divorced twice and told me the circumstances. Ordinarily, I might have felt wary, but Twice shared his story and seemed really sincere in his desire to clear the air and be honest. I trusted my friend and was looking forward to our date.

We were circling around looking for parking on the Upper West Side. As we whizzed down 72nd street, I thought I saw Singular seated in a store window. *Must be my imagination. Why am I letting him intrude on my thoughts?* I should focus on Twice.

Twice found a spot, we parked, and started walking. You guessed it. We walked straight towards the window where Singular and his date – whom I recognized as well – were seated having an animated conversation. *Another coincidence?* Wow. I was rattled. I tripped as we entered the restaurant. I told Twice I'd like to say hello to the couple in the window. I wasn't going to spend an hour pretending I didn't see or know Singular. When I was younger, I'd often do just that because the social bumbling of a blind date was all I could handle. In fact, I had done it on my first date with Singular when I spotted a classmate. But now I was older, knew the woman he was with, and felt comfortable approaching them.

We walked over to say hi and make quick introductions. Singular's eyebrows shot up as he sputtered, "Hello." He hadn't seen us enter the restaurant. He eyed my date, was surprised to see I knew his, and then Twice and I quickly retreated to our own table. But my mind was in a whirl. *He's out with her? Who set him up with her? She's very nice, but I'm much more suitable!* I was trying to make small talk with Twice, but my mind was not focused at my own table. It was at the table in the window. I was running into Singular quite often. It seemed he appeared everywhere. *Was God trying to push us towards each other?* At this point, I was convinced, but why wasn't Singular? My date with Twice flew by, but I could not remember a thing other than that I had seen Singular from the car, before we ever entered the place.

Twice wanted another date, but I was a fool. I allowed this Singular diversion to divert me enough to say no to another date, even though there was no good reason for me to do that.

More dates followed. I agreed to meet Ponytail, a friend of a friend's brother. The friends were all religious in a conventional way, so I was expecting a conventional religious man. But he showed up with a *kippah* on top of a ponytail. I was taken by surprise to see this hippie-like fellow. I would've felt far more comfortable meeting him in the city rather than at my doorstep for all the neighbors to ogle. He was a very nice person, but this was not the lifestyle for me. Next.

Next was the guy who acted above it all, as though being with me was beneath him. But when a dog crossed our path, he suddenly yelped like a frightened child. By this time, I had conquered my fear and saw dogs for the lovable creatures they are. This man's phobia made me feel like his protector. It was not a great feeling.

He then wanted to exert his masculinity by hiring a taxi to take me home from the city. I suppose it was the gentlemanly thing to do. I insisted the subway was okay because I had been in this situation in the past. Having no idea what the meter would read by the time the cab reached my door, he shoved a fistful of bills into my hand, in full view of the cabbie. Like he was paying me for services. I wanted a sinkhole to open and swallow me. Next.

It was Purim. I usually went to my parents for the festive meal, but this year Singular invited me to join him at the Chassidic family hosting him. His family was secular, so for many of the holidays he was a *ben bayis* – a regular guest of this family. My parents would be having

123

their grandchildren over. They had heard so much about Singular, they too felt I should go. It may help move things along.

Then Singular told me the unthinkable. He had a date after our dinner. *Is he for real? Why do I keep ignoring his words?* He repeatedly had told me I was not the one, but I felt that actions speak louder than words, and his actions betrayed his feelings. My friends all saw it too. Why invite me at all if I was of no interest to him? What was he truly thinking?

I was at a crossroads. *Should I let him make a fool of me? Should I drop the whole thing?* This was not some guy I had a schoolgirl crush on. This was a man who had caught me unawares. He was not someone I had expected to become anything more than a blind date, but over time, God had continually made our paths cross. Gradually, friendship, respect, and love had blossomed. He had grown, little by little, into someone I could picture myself with in the future. He was a man with the intellect, sense of humor, kindness, and *hashkafah* level to match my own. Others also commented on how much sense it would make, or how we seemed to suit each other. Was he afraid of commitment? Confused? Conflicted?

I thought it over. I had heard so much about his host family and I was curious. Perhaps I should meet them. Maybe they understood Singular better than I did. Maybe they could help me walk away for good or, better yet, help him come to his senses. So, I said yes.

I prepared a cute *shalach manos* with a banana bird. I had painted eyes on the banana and let the "bird's beak" stick out of the little shopping bag packed with goodies. When Singular picked me up and I handed it to him, his eyes shone in merriment as he held the bag aloft and admired my little creation. He drove us to his "family" and when we entered, the place was packed with people. They had lots of kids, neighbors, and friends over. He dragged me over to the rebbetzin and said, "This is my friend! Look at this bird she made for me!" He was showing off me (and my *shalach manos*) with so much pride, as though I were his new bride.

The party was nice and the family was friendly. After a while,

Singular whispered to me, "I'm leaving for my date." With the forbearance of a saint, I said, "What do you want me to say when they ask me where you've gone?"

"Oh, I told them I have a date. Don't worry!" and with that he disappeared.

A short while later, the rebbetzin asked me, "Where is Singular?"

She was about to learn how inexplicable the bachelor male mind was. "On a date," I said, realizing she would find his actions unimaginable.

"What do you mean 'on a date?' Aren't *you* his date?" which segued into the conversation I needed to have with her. The one where she confirmed what I already knew. There was something very, very wrong. If a man is interested, he runs towards you, not away. I knew I had to accept it and move on. I'd had an interesting Purim *seudah*, and my curiosity about this family had been satisfied. They were lovely.

A year later, one of Singular's friends asked me out. I was not interested, but I said yes. I suppose subconsciously I wanted some sort of connection to Singular. But we weren't on the same page about anything, not even where to go. And we never made it to a second date.

However, Singular must've heard about it because, the next thing I knew, Singular was calling me. Again. It was clear he was upset I had gone out with this man. *Why be jealous if he didn't want to date me? Did he truly think us eminently unsuitable for each other?* It was Purim again, he was going to his "family" and wanted to know where I'd be. I was going to my parents' house this time. I asked him if he'd like to stop by to meet my parents. He agreed to stop by.

When he arrived, he handed me a simple *shalach manos*, in all earnestness. It was nothing more than an unadorned, thin white paper plate with a small green lollipop (was it a leftover green lollipop that no one else wanted?) and some baby carrots. There were no home-baked goodies, no banana bird, no store-bought pastry, no ribbon, no card, no creative effort put into it at all, other than that he travelled to my neck of the woods. Yet this cheap paper plate made me so happy.

What mattered to me was that he'd shown up. I invited him in but he claimed he was pressed for time. *But hadn't the whole point been to meet my parents?*

I believe he was intimidated. Perhaps it signified too much to him, or he worried it would signify too much to me and my parents. Sometimes his words hinted that he feared my father was a towering religious fanatic who would not accept him. Despite my assurances that he was not at all like that, Singular refused to come upstairs. Again, the emotion and the soft smile just did not reconcile with his words that pushed me away. Despite his words, he had come. Going out on that date with his friend had paid off, after all. Or not. I was still not his *basherte*.

Them

Them. There were too many of them: the hundreds of men I'd spoken to, flirted with, tried to impress, tried to avoid, went out with, or was dumped, hurt, or humiliated by. The men I had let down, disappointed, angered. The men who were shy, talkative, awkward, pleasant, boring, exciting, disheveled, sharp, cheap, extravagant, nice, angry, violent, or just plain nuts. There had even been a Moroccan tour guide who seemed serious when he asked whether my father would accept ten camels for my hand in marriage.

There were more of Them than I'd ever imagined there would be. Before my first date, I distinctly remember not feeling ready for marriage and worrying about what I'd do if I too, met the "right" one immediately as so many of my classmates seemed to do. I had naively thought that my issue would be meeting my *basherte* too soon. I never imagined the opposite would be true.

You'd think the odds would be in my favor, but there was a problem or two. For one thing, there were even more of Us, the women. As happens in the game of musical chairs, when the music stopped, I'd race to sit and find all the chairs occupied with none left for me. It seemed that in the dating game too – if we can call it a game – when a decent man interested me, it was as though the music stopped abruptly. A line of women reached him before I managed to, and usually he wound up marrying one of them.

If I could watch myself on my dates, I'm sure I could point out most of my own mistakes, faux pas, character flaws, and foolish things I've said or done, but it's easy to rationalize our own behaviors while looking critically at those of others. I wasn't in front of a mirror watching myself. I had a front row seat to Them.

I kept a poker face and ignored the sniffling, itching, scratching, rubbing, snorting, coughing, and twitching of Them. I tried to keep my food down, despite dandruff, snot, spit, beard hairs falling into their plates. I listened to monologues, speeches, tirades, outbursts, confessions, *divrei Torah*, stories, and jokes, or just put up with thick silence when my date had nothing to say and I tired of carrying the conversation.

It's not easy for Them either – especially not on blind dates. They have to plan, pay, drive, find parking, or hire a car service, meet the roommates, or parents. They have to come upstairs or wait downstairs or ask to use the restroom, or hold themselves in till their destination. It's all for a woman they haven't met and may not like. I get it.

That's why I tried really hard to be a good date and pleasant company for Them. I tried to smile, look nice, laugh at their jokes, tell good stories. I tried. But some of them didn't make it easy. They made a face the moment they laid eyes on me. They became very taciturn and quiet, made no eye contact. Others missed cues of disinterest and put me on the spot asking for a second date.

There was a coworker much, much older than me, who asked a third party to ask me whether I was interested. In order to help him save face, we pretended I had been asked if I was available, and I had said no before ever hearing his name. But he was clearly angry and ignored my hellos for the next few months.

Some people do marry one of their first dates. Do they count themselves lucky? Do they regret their choices? Know they'd make the same choice if they were ten years older? Even when it seems simple, it may not always be. I used to envy the simplicity of the animal world. It seems animals are guided by instinct, pair off, and mate. But I learned that it's not all that easy in the animal world either. Some males must work to attract and impress the females with their beauty or song. Other males fight off their competition in bloody battles. Like us, they have to impress, compete or battle for their mates – but on the other hand, they don't play phone tag or contend with matchmakers.

PART FOUR

I Am with Him in Distress (Psalms 91:15)

עמו אנכי בצרה (תהילים צ"א:טו)

A Big Question Mark

One date, from out of town, arrived with a list of 100 questions. *What could those questions possibly be?* The moment he alerted me to his 100-questions list, I wanted to go home, but I humored him to see what he'd ask. I promised myself I wouldn't answer anything too personal, as I was sure I wasn't going on a second date with him. At least there wouldn't be awkward silences during our meal. He started with the banal "How many sisters and brothers do you have?" and continued with increasingly absurd queries till his last question.

"This is the most important question of all," he said, just as we finished eating. I could not imagine what he could possibly ask me after all those other inane questions and how it could be the most important. *Hmmm. Was he going to propose? Ha! He won't be happy with the answer to that question!*

"Would you be open to getting married in Chicago – where my grandmother lives – as she would not be able to travel anywhere for our wedding?" *Our wedding? Whoa! He skipped the proposal and is already planning the wedding!*

"We're on our first date, don't you think this is all a bit premature?" I asked. One of the few questions I managed that evening.

But he surprised me with another question. *Weren't 100 questions more than enough?* "On the scale of one to ten, with ten being the highest, how would you rate this date?" *Oh wow. Really?*

To save face – his, not mine – I avoided his question by answering with another question, "Do you really need to ask?" and smiled. I think he went home sure it was a ten, and I went home sure it didn't even rate a one. It was an abysmal zero.

That evening I was left with my constant question for God. *Why?*

It's Not so Black and White

In my thirties, I attended many *Shabbatonim*. At the next one, the moment I walked into the synagogue Friday night, my heart sank. Many were men I had already met or were much too old for me. I was disappointed but there was nothing to do but make the most of the next twenty-five hours. I tried to carry awkward conversations that stalled. I greeted people and smiled. It would be a painful weekend. *This too shall pass.* I realized that while my twenties had not been easy, dating in my thirties was just going to get tougher.

"*Lo tov hayos haadam levado* – It is not good for man to be alone," the Bible tells us. The adage seemed consistently true. I was often advised to marry a man and "fix him up," but I needed to marry someone I liked, respected, and befriended.

Was I being picky or difficult? I didn't think so because all I wanted was someone who shared my values to whom I could talk easily. A friend. I could easily converse with non-Jewish stock boys in the fruit store, bus drivers, or mailmen. Why was it so difficult to talk to Jewish doctors, accountants, business owners? In our determined quest for marriage, did every conversation have to be so loaded, pointed, and uncomfortable?

I spent the evening smiling, speaking with women, and trying to talk to men. The other women felt the same despair and were whispering about how few of the men were remotely marriageable. As it was Shabbos, there was no traveling home. We were stuck at our hosts' homes and had to come back to *shul* for our next meal.

The next morning, I came to *shul* and prayed to God to fix whatever the problem was. The synagogue was crowded with its regulars. After services, it was bittersweet to see appealing men mingling at the *Kiddush* buffet because we knew that they were probably married congregants. The single women wondered. *How did they meet their spouse? When did they meet? How did we get left out?*

I sidled up to the buffet, not wanting to watch all the couples. At least I'd enjoy the *cholent* and salads. Suddenly I noticed a well-dressed black man in a suit and *kippah* next to me, trying to scoop some *kugel* onto his plate. He smiled pleasantly. I was confused. I hadn't seen him at the meal Friday night. *He must have a difficult time dating.* He asked me where I'm from and if I had ever been to this area before. It was instantly obvious that he knew how to engage with a woman in a friendly manner. *Wow I didn't expect to meet someone like this.* But before I had a chance to weigh the situation another moment, he said, "My wife and I daven here."

He's married. I should've known!

Other married men I had met made sure to mention their wives immediately. It struck me as going beyond setting boundaries. In many cases, it appeared to be an arrogant belief of my non-existent interest in them. In this case, though I felt foolish for my assumption, it was warranted. This was, after all, a singles' *Shabbaton*.

"I can't believe what I'm seeing. It breaks my heart to see this crowd. There are two distinct populations in here," he said, as he scanned the room, nodding in disbelief. "The women clearly outshine the men. I'm so sorry that you came to my *shul* for this."

"Yeah, it's very discouraging," I said, as his cute son ran up to him and tugged at his leg. I could tell by looking at his beautiful child's mixed-raced features and hair that his wife must be white. *How had he met her? Had he been born Jewish or converted?*

Well at least he's sympathetic. He gets it.

131

Matchmakers would try to explain that married men are more attractive to single women because they're unavailable, or that they seem more personable because their wives "fixed" them up. But I didn't buy it. That was an insult to men as a group. Not every man has to be told to wear clean clothes or stand straight. Plenty of men figure out the basics on their own. I'm sure marriage does mature men, but the reason personable males do get married is because they are able to attract a woman in the first place.

The men in this ballroom were repelling women, not attracting them. This man understood. I could see him brooding on this disturbing scene. Then he began, "My wife and I were high school sweethearts, so we never had to go through this..."

Oh, break my heart some more.

"Because of her, I became interested in Judaism, wanted to convert, and we became *frum* together. Then when it came to marriage, we already knew each other and were there for each other. But sometimes I wonder..." he chewed his lip.

I waited.

"I wonder if I were still single and came to this *Shabbaton* whether any of the women here would give me a chance." I waited some more. *I don't know. I really don't know. But it's a moot point. He's happily married.*

It clearly weighed on him, as though by a stroke of pure luck, he had missed this painful fate of attending these awful single events. "I know this is a loaded question, but I do wonder. Would you ever have considered marrying a black man?"

No, I had not, but I had also never met a frum, personable, and thoughtful black man before now. I don't know.

"I'd like to think that I would, but it's not that simple," I finally responded.

Standing there in a room full of men I could not relate to, he was head and shoulders above them. I think I would want to date this man if he were single. I didn't know how my family or friends would react or whether I could handle being stared at while at his side. I didn't know whether that would mean subjecting children to the difficulties of being mixed-raced in *frum* society. I didn't know if I could follow all the way through to marriage, but I think I would date him to get to know him better and take it one step at a time. For me, character means so much more than skin color, and he had loads of character. But society is judgmental and I wasn't sure I could deal with that.

Just then his wife found him. He introduced us and shortly thereafter we wished each other *Good Shabbos*. He wished me luck. I watched them leave as a family while I stayed with all the other singles trying to navigate our way to marriage.

His question remained behind for a long while after. I really didn't know what I would have done. It's not so black and white.

Spider Web

The world was changing rapidly. Before World War II, my eastern European father had lived in a rural village home with a wood stove and an outhouse. My western European mother had lived in the suburbs of Paris. Her family did have indoor plumbing, and the family had preserved food in their cold cellar. The only phone in town had been at the post office. In 1949, my father arrived by ship via Boston. He remembered being astonished to see so many bright city lights as they approached the harbor. Only a decade later, my mother flew to the States as air travel had become more mainstream than ships.

We grew up with the new modern conveniences of the day. We had kitchen appliances – a green refrigerator (in vogue at the time), a corded phone, a box radio, and a black and white TV that looked like a piece of fancy furniture. Though we didn't have a car, my uncle had an aqua-colored winged sedan and took us out on outings to the local park for "fresh air." We thought the world had modernized. Then, over the next decade or two, new gadgets came out.

The rich girls in class showed off their digital watches and calculators while the rest of us gathered round to inspect these new gizmos in awe. We had spent hours memorizing the times table, and now this little magic pad could do it for us instantly. Stores replaced their manual cash registers with digital machines. Supermarkets could scan your items. The library no longer had to photocopy our library loans. The bank tellers were replaced with ATM machines. Record players were overtaken by Sony Walkmans, roller skates by Rollerblades. Inch by inch, gadget by gadget, the world was changing.

As a programming major, I had to submit my program via monitors that could display text only and would transmit it to punch cards. At my first job, I worked on mechanical paste-up layouts and a typesetting machine that was considered state-of-the-art. It was a big upgrade from the way printers had set type letter by letter with metal molds way before my time. I would set galleys of text, then cut them apart and wax them so I could manually paste them into columns. I used a huge stat camera to copy photographs which I pasted into place as well. I had taken a summer course before college to learn all this and the teacher had told us, "They are talking about a machine that will be able to combine text and photos all in one." The entire class scoffed at this impossibility! Even in an age where the seeming impossibility of a plane suspended in air, or sounds traveling over radio waves was normal, we still could not envision this miracle "machine."

A short year or two later, PCs and Macs were introduced to the consumer. Computers were in and machines were out. The world spun its technological web faster and faster till the actual world wide web (www.) was born. People did not know what to make of it. There were very few websites, and no website-building templates. The agency I worked for put up one page with their profile and contact information. One partner didn't see the point, as our contact info was already available in the Yellow Pages phone book.

Day by day, new ideas popped up in the internet world, whether it was blogging, shopping, news, or searching for long-lost relatives. The world was waking up to its unlimited possibilities.

Till one day there was internet dating. I was intrigued. I signed up on the first Jewish dating website. There were only a few intrepid members, and almost all of them were men. Hardly any women were comfortable with this idea, which to my mind put the odds greatly in my favor. Hardly anyone posted a picture. We were all camera-shy and accustomed to "blind" dating and risk-taking. Exposing one's life online was not yet the norm. People were still modest and private. I could be old-fashioned with other things, but when it came to this website, I was an eager participant.

Perhaps looking for a *shidduch* online still seemed illicit at this early stage, but I saw opportunity. It would introduce me to men across the United States and the world, whom I most likely would not otherwise meet through ordinary channels.

My friends cautioned me, "You don't *know* who these random strangers are!" as though they truly believed every matchmaker fully vetted every guy sent their way. I had been blind-dating random strangers all the time. Just because a man called a matchmaker didn't mean he couldn't be completely off the wall – as many of my dates had proven to be. Besides, we could investigate and ask for references in exactly the same way we did for our blind dates, but the pool of men would be greater.

There was no Google, Facebook, or Instagram. This was before you could know everything you thought you wanted to know about a person without meeting him – when we still invested in the other person and dived in, taking the chance.

I didn't have any issue with online dating at all. In fact, I liked having the ability to vet out the candidates. I could gauge the depth of their sincerity to marry. The fact is that my dates did improve. If a man made it past his profile and past a phone call to an actual date, it would automatically up the chances that our time spent together would be somewhat pleasant and purposeful. I was ready.

The problem I did not anticipate would be how far this technology would spin its web. Everything can be a force for good, or not. Soon internet dating would become as sticky as a spider's web.

Miles Apart

The good thing about internet dating was cutting out the *shadchan*. The bad thing about internet dating was cutting out the *shadchan*. On the positive side, if I sensed a man was really not for me, I could wish him well, click "send," and it would be over. I wouldn't have to explain and defend to a third party, or cave in and acquiesce to a date I didn't want just to please the person setting me up. So that was good. There is some truth to "you never know" till you meet a person, yet there are times when you just know it's a "no." I had been dating long enough not to want to date just anyone or go on trial as a defendant every time I chose to turn someone down.

On the other hand, if I was interested in someone and emailing him for a bit, and he'd suddenly vanish into thin air, I had no way of knowing what had happened, whether he had been hit by a car or struck by lightning. Without a matchmaker to follow up for me, I was sure that man after man had been cut down by some catastrophe like the soldiers on Normandy Beach. The odds were of course, that unlike the brave soldiers, these men were cowards who had lost interest and lacked the courage to tell me so.

Despite all that, one of the major advantages of internet dating was opening the pool of available men geographically. I could meet men who lived in towns without too many single women. I reasoned that I'd ask for references so I wouldn't be left stranded blindly.

Time and time again, the men would ask me to visit them, instead of offering to come see me. Although I mourned the lack of chivalry, I did not view myself as desperate for visiting them. They had reasonable explanations – jobs they couldn't get away from, no vacation time, kids they couldn't leave. They didn't pay for my tickets, but I didn't expect them to because they barely knew me. And I assumed they would return the favor at some point. Only in hindsight, I realized I had been a fool.

Conman had invited me to his city, put me up at a neighbor, and we had gone out for Shabbos meals together. I met his parents and his rabbi. All this made things more intense. For me, the experience was a sweet taste of what coupledom could feel like and I relished it. People assumed we were engaged or would be soon. I did too. Yet he was dating several women at the same time, unbeknownst to me.

It turned out I had invested time and money while he simultaneously dated someone else and subsequently married her. I was so upset at the news, that I called his mother and rabbi, who both told me I was better off without him. *If they truly believed that, why hadn't they warned me earlier?* Conman had told me he had been engaged once before, but his mother asked me "Didn't he tell you about his other engagements?"

"Um, noooooooo!"

His own mother told me there had been several and that I deserved better than her son, and sure enough, he ended up divorced a year or two later.

Another out-of-towner, Shame, dragged me around to all his friends for Shabbos and seemed excited to show me off. He was a BT and seemed smart, talented, engaging. I enjoyed our conversations, and felt we shared the same *hashkafah*. Then he surprised me, saying, "It's a shame it doesn't work, we get along so well."

I had no idea what he meant by that. "So, make it work," I said.

Shame broke up with me, but kept calling and calling. My mother warned me not to allow myself to get hurt. I didn't know what to do because I did hope it could still work out. If he wasn't interested, I didn't want him to call me, but what if I just wasn't the person he had envisioned marrying? Was he using me, or warming up to me? I wasn't sure.

Then one day he called and asked for my address.

"Why? Are you coming to see me?

"Not exactly, but a matchmaker is setting me up with someone who I think lives on your street."

"What? Who is it?"

It was someone that was in no way, shape, or form his *basherte*. That hurt. He clearly was not interested in me. He also hadn't flown in for me, though we had spent hours talking. But now he would fly in for a blind date? I felt ashamed for having been so foolish.

"I won't tell you what to do, but I'll be very surprised if you marry her."

"But a matchmaker matched us!" he said. He had always met women on his own in his former life and he was very unaware of how random blind dates could be.

After he had flown in and dated her, he called to complain. "I can't believe they would have me fly across the country for someone I had nothing in common with."

He was completely oblivious to my feelings. I didn't want to be "friends" with him. I thought he was talented and interesting, but I didn't like the way I was being treated.

Weeks later, he called again bemoaning a woman he was dating who had kids. That was the slap that woke me right up. I wasn't a woman to him. I was a sounding board.

"Why are you calling me to complain about this? You chose to date her, not me, so please stop calling." I had finally come to my senses.

Months later, I answered my phone and a woman introduced herself as Shame's *kallah*.

He's engaged?? What a way to find out! Why would he give her my number without my permission? I was very upset at the unexpected news and very uncomfortable. This man had broken my heart and he had his fiancée call me without warning me ahead of time.

She was very gabby and thought she was being friendly, while all I wanted was to hang up.

"I heard sooooo much about you, and you seem sooooo wonderful and I know a really great, great guy. I want to set you two up." I'm sure she thought she was being charitable, but she was completely clueless about how this news affected me. I wasn't interested in her suggestions.

"Sorry, I'm not comfortable with this," I said. I knew how things had turned out in the past when a dumper had set me up with a consolation date. The new date had never measured up to the dumper. It just made me feel worse about being dumped. Based on past experiences, this was NOT a good idea – not from the dumper, and definitely not from his fiancée.

"Why ever not? You never know where a *shidduch* can come from!" she exclaimed cheerily. "Please don't shoot yourself in the foot. He's a really, really GREAT guy!"

Yes, but she hadn't gotten engaged to this "great" guy. She had gotten engaged to Shame! Perhaps the intention was pure, but the way they were going about it was not sensitive at all. I was upset. Somehow, I got off the phone. *What had he seen in her?*

A couple of days later Shame called. His soothing calm voice was familiar, but I reminded myself that he had chosen to marry someone else. I didn't want to talk to him. I don't know how he did it, or why, but he convinced me to allow this gentleman from Atlanta to call me.

When the call came, our conversation was stilted and speaking with him just brought up fresh waves of grief over Shame and his *kallah*. I didn't need this painful reminder. I didn't want this man to fly in to see me. It would put unwanted pressure on me. It was best if I moved on and put this all behind me. I told him the truth.

"I'm sure you're a nice guy, but I don't think it will work out," I said. "The happy couple foisted this on me, but I did try to tell them the timing was not good for me now." I could tell he was disappointed. But I couldn't go through with this.

"Well, that's just fine with me," he retorted. "I would never move to New York anyhow!"

I thought his remark uncalled for as I had never asked him to move. He was being petulant in his attempt to save face. This confirmed what I already believed – we were miles apart in more ways than one.

"Good luck then," I said. We hung up.

A year or so later, he broke his word and moved to NY. He met and married someone who lived right on my street. *What were the odds of that?* In fact, he had been set up by another party with the very woman Shame had flown in to date.

God has a sense of humor, but I wasn't amused.

Stirring the Pot

I was set up with a gynecologist who spent the entire date telling me he knew more about women's bodies than I did. *You don't know what it feels like to cramp every month, have out-of-whack raging hormones, or pass out in a faint! You don't know what it's like to schedule your life around a calendar and have that timetable betray you so that you wind up opposite a pompous fool on the worst, most painful, jittery day of the month.* I was fed up but I let Gynecologist go on and prove how smart he was. I summoned every last ounce of energy to suffer through the date and his thesis on female anatomy. Marrying a guy who explored women's bodies on a regular basis wasn't appealing to me.

Over a Shabbos meal, I whined to a friend and her husband about my awful dates. Her husband said, "There are plenty of nice men out there. Can't be too hard to find someone. You're not trying hard enough."

Said the guy who got married in his forties! I challenged him, "Ok then, find me a date if you think it's so simple!"

He found me one. Very quickly. He found him right in *shul*. Aimless called and sounded off, weird, couldn't finish his sentences. Something was very, very wrong. I would go out on this date so I could see exactly who this expert thought he was setting me up with. Bad decision. I should've cancelled.

Aimless told me he didn't have a car. Most men outside of Manhattan either had a car or access to one they could borrow, so I had a hint of things to come. But as he lived in the neighborhood, I agreed to meet him at a restaurant near my home.

When he showed up, I recognized him. He was not a bad-looking fellow, but he was another one of those guys one notices circling in the neighborhood like Doc. Unfortunately, the restaurant I chose had small tables crowded together. At the table right next to ours sat an older married couple who could overhear our conversation. This made me uneasy, as I feared Aimless would embarrass me. My fears were not unfounded.

He began by telling me he was unemployed; he had lost his apartment; moved into his mother's basement; he was a loner. This was bad. *He fits the profile of a mass murderer.* He also did not finish any of his sentences.

"I had a car but…" and then his red eyes would shift from side to side, scanning the room.

"But what?" I prompted.

"It was repossessed…" he sighed. I was praying the couple inches away from us weren't listening in.

Gee, his eyes are red. He can't finish his sentences. Wonder what he's on.

"Do you…" and he lost his train of thought.

"Do I what?"

"Um… do you, do you smoke… pot?" he finished as casually as other guys would ask whether I liked olives.

"Do I what?" I was sure I heard wrong.

"Do you… do you smoke pot?" All I could focus on was the nice married couple sitting next to us and praying they were engrossed in their own conversation. This was beyond humiliating. Our conversation had been moronic, and now this question?

I snapped, "Why would you ask me a question like that?"

"You… you look like you do," he said in all sincerity.

I was fuming. I thought perhaps he was on medication, but he was a pothead. Even worse, he was clearly high.

What a loser! My friend's husband is some expert on dating! Somebody is going to have some explaining to do!

Yet what did it matter if my friend's husband was wrong and I was right? I was the one stuck on this appalling date. I needed to wrap this up, go home and beg God never to do this to me again. *Did God do this? Or was it my friend's husband?* Ok I would beg God never to allow my friend's husband or anyone else to do this to me. I would pour my heart and my eyes out. I told Aimless I needed to get home.

"Now?" he asked.

"Yes now."

"Can we do this again?"

Is he kidding me? I was blunt. "No."

"Why not?" he asked.

"Because I don't date stoned guys. That's why." I hoped the couple two inches to my right realized I am *so* not with this guy.

"Aw, come on. I emptied my wallet out for you!"

I guess next week's pot supply won't be coming. This is downright cringeworthy.

"I just need to get home."

"Can I walk you home?"

"No."

"Why?"

"I don't walk the streets with potheads. Good night." The thought of Aimless tottering alongside me was very unappealing.

I gathered my things and left.

My friend's husband never again told me I wasn't trying hard enough. He had stirred the pot once and the recipe had been a disaster.

Court Rules

Judging a guy by his job was as futile as judging a guy by any other parameter. I assumed a date with Judge would at least portend an intelligent conversation, but I was mistaken once again. We hadn't said much to each other when the waiter handed us our menus with a flourish and a twinkle in his eye. The contrast between the waiter's and the date's personality was glaring.

Judge scanned the menu and then casually asked, "So what's your favorite TV show?" *What a way for a judge to start a conversation.* I could not believe it. Surely there were many other far more interesting topics we could tackle.

"Uh, can we talk about something else please?"

He didn't seem to grasp how unappealing this was as a first conversation with a stranger. "But why?" he persisted. "My last date also didn't want to talk about TV."

"Well, that should clue you in," I remarked, thinking how speaking about previous dates should be as off-limits as speaking about TV.

"But it's better than politics and religion," he smiled at his own joke.

"Surely a judge can think of something more intelligent to speak about," I said.

"My last date told me that when she will be married, curled up to her spouse, I'll be curled up around my TV," he said. *My goodness! How is this man a judge? Had he no discretion whatsoever?*

"Now why would you tell me something like that? Don't you realize how pathetic that makes you sound?" I was aggravated by this nonsensical talk. The fresh-faced waiter who came for our orders overheard us. He raised his brow and smiled at me. I glanced at him and turned away. He had to realize this was an awful blind date.

Judge pouted and told me to order a soup. Another "order a soup" guy. This time I wasn't hungry and was very happy to oblige and just get this over with.

Nodding toward the waiter, he whispered, "You know that guy makes tips. He probably can't afford to eat in a place like this." I ignored that remark and we stumbled through the date. I could imagine him thinking, "*No wonder she's not married – making eyes at a young loser like that.*" I just sipped my soup. I didn't care anymore. The *young loser* clearly had more looks, brains, and charm than this judge.

After our meal, I excused myself from the table and asked the waiter where the restroom was. The waiter who had seen me suffer through this bowl of soup pointed to the stairs at the back and whispered, "Take the stairs back there, go up, left, down and around to the subway, and get yourself home." It was a moment of comic relief in a sorry situation. He smiled reassuringly, but I felt like laughing and crying at the same time. "Don't worry, you'll be home soon." I was just relieved that he understood I wasn't *with* this man.

The date was almost over. I would survive it and go home. This judge probably knew the rules of court but sadly, almost nothing about the rules of courtship.

Treading Water

Water was a divorced man a professional *shadchan* had pushed on me. I didn't have much information, but as my bachelor dates were going so awry, I hoped this divorced man at least had some practice speaking to women. As I soon found out, he did indeed – very condescendingly. We had made a date for one evening after work and I had no idea what he had in mind. I usually like to know ahead of time whether we were going out to eat or not. If not, I'd grab a quick bite ahead of time, and if yes, I'd check whether we'd have meat or dairy. So, when I got into the car, as he had not mentioned it before, I politely inquired as to what we were going to be doing. He snapped, "The man makes the decision. You'll see when we get there." *Oh! Get me out of here. Now.*

The boat had not left the dock and was already sunk. This was another date where I'd be treading water just to survive. I remained silent when what I wanted to do was stop the date immediately. I would try to be polite for the matchmaker's sake, even for his sake. It certainly was not doing me any good. He drove at ten miles an hour or slower. I could bike faster. I wondered, why? There was tension in the car. *Why would he want to prolong it? How long would this date last?* It was crawling along at a snail's pace and had not even started. I snuck a peek at my watch.

"Why are you looking at your watch?" Water snapped again. *He's creepier than creepy.*

"Why are you driving at ten miles per hour?" I retorted. I had learned that answering a question with a question was a good way to deflect answering. It had taken me years to learn that just because someone asked me a question, like how old I was, I was under no obligation to answer.

Turned out he had no idea where he was going. I quickly suggested the closest restaurant I could think of. It was not a good choice. Again, the tables were seated way too close for my comfort when conversing with a stranger like this. At the next table, inches away, was a cute, young Sephardic couple who looked like they were enjoying their meal and each other's company. The atmosphere was romantic, the tables candlelit. I was filled with sorrow and not a little envy. *Why is this my lot in life? Why am I sitting here with a creep? How did they meet?*

We washed for our bread, ordered sushi as an appetizer, and looked over the menu for entrées. He was talking and I remained silent. I was no longer interested in anything Water had to say. It was all nonsense. He started talking about the kosher dietary restrictions on water, of all things. I knew there really aren't any. For anyone concerned, perhaps water consumed on Passover could be somewhat of an issue, but even then, not really. Filtered or bottled water is always kosher. But when I said so, he pushed back argumentatively, so I let it go and let him rant on. I gazed at my menu, not him.

"You are not listening!" he hissed across the table. I saw our neighbors glancing furtively at us.

I didn't respond, which infuriated him more. I just looked at him. I was weighing what to do or say.

"Do you want me to take you home right now?" he threatened me, as though I were a child, as though that would be punishment rather than salvation. I'd had it.

"Yes, I do," I said evenly. That was not at all the answer he expected.

He flung the menu my way, startling me, and said, "I'll go tell them not to fill our sushi order." Then he stormed off to the sushi bar at the front of the restaurant behind me. We would still have to pay for the bread, drinks, and little appetizer salads on the table. We would still have to *bentch*. But hopefully, soon after, it would be over. My emotions were all over the place – anger, sadness, envy, depression, hopelessness. Dating could at times be fun, but for me, especially at times like this, it was torture, in this case water torture. Unbearable.

The sweet girl at the next table leaned over. "I think your date left," she whispered.

"It's a blind date." *I needed to clear that up.* "He went to pay."

"He left," she and her date both said.

"What do you mean 'he left'?"

"We just saw him leave." He hadn't paid nor *bentched*. It was inconceivable.

"Maybe he wanted to make a call and went outside for privacy?" I was giving him the benefit of the doubt. I was in denial. *The guy was crazy, but was he that crazy?*

"I guess you heard him arguing about the *kashrus* of water," I said. They both nodded solemnly. I could sense their empathy. I asked how they had met and was astonished at the irony. Here I was with a guy I had been "matched" with who was no match at all, while they had found each other quite by accident. The guy was trying to call his friend, misdialed, got the girl. They were both young, Sephardic, religious Jews and single – and here they were. God is a better matchmaker than his earthly counterparts. What a story!

Soon another empathetic middle-aged couple came over, "We can't believe that he ditched you. We'd be glad to give you a ride home, but we just arrived. If you don't mind waiting, we'll take you home." I politely declined. It was beginning to sink in that he was indeed gone. Well, on the bright side that meant I wouldn't have to share another snail's-pace car ride with him.

The maitre d' came over as well. I offered to pay for the meals we had ordered, but she wouldn't allow it.

"You have this jerk's number?"

I had it at home.

"Well, you go on home and call me with his number. I'll track him down and make him pay. In the meantime, I'll call a car service for you."

It was a small restaurant. Everyone had heard and seen what he had done. Everyone was kind to me and trying to soften the horribly awkward situation. I was grateful.

As it took some time to figure out that he had left, accept all my "condolences" and order a car, forty-five minutes had elapsed since the moment Water had stormed out in a huff. A car honked.

The maitre d' alerted me that my ride had arrived, then placed her hand on my arm before I could get to the door, and motioned for me to wait. She had spotted him before I did. The door opened. Water was there. He did not look my way at all. He turned to the maitre d' and said, "I forgot to *bentch*," and walked back to our table.

The maitre d' and I eyed each other, eyebrows raised. I was floored. He had also forgotten to pay and forgotten to be a mensch. Why was he concerned about saying *Birchas Hamazon* but not concerned about basic respect for his fellow man? It was outrageous.

She whispered, "Call me later, anyhow," hugged me, and guided me to the door.

The driver of the car was a young, secular Russian Jew and I told him my story. He was incredulous about what had happened, and was warm and funny. He cheered me up and I laughed all the way home.

Why were guys who did not fit my profile at all so easy to speak with? Why were my dates so awful? I asked God these questions all the time because I did not understand. Were all the good *frum* guys married? Where were they? I struggled with this. I literally had to turn down men who I found interesting and nice because they did not share my Jewish values, while at the same time I had to run away from men who did share my values on paper, weren't compatible with me in any meaningful way. I begged God not to test me this way. I would be happier accepting my fate as a single woman than suffering through this sort of ordeal again.

When I arrived home, I called the maitre d'. She told me he had finished *bentching*, then handed her his credit card without a word. What he didn't grasp was that *derech eretz kadma l'Torah*. Basic human courtesy precedes Torah and certainly precedes the laws of *kashrus* on water.

I was home alone. I was numb after this evening. I had no words. The only language left in me tonight was the language of water. Salt water. I went to bed and cried it all out.

Stood Up and Collapse Down

I thought I cried it all out, but there were plenty more where those tears came from. Another man suggested we meet in Bryant Park after work and then decide where to go from there. I was savvy enough to know this meant he wanted to check me out first and then determine if I was worth a coffee or a dinner. When people ask me why I would go forward with a date when I already felt doubtful before it started, I would remind them that I wanted to get married and the pickings were slim. I was trying to give it a chance. Once again, I tried when I shouldn't have.

I arrived at the park on a glorious summer evening and spotted my date from a distance. I normally approach and say "Hi. How are you?" But he approached me and didn't say hello, didn't ask my name, didn't say a word about the beautiful weather. He looked at me as though I were the ugliest woman he had ever seen and spat out, "How old are you, anyhow?"

It took me exactly one split-second to realize I would never marry someone that nasty. What I said no longer mattered. From what I read on his profile, I was four years younger than him, and if he had lied, the gap would be even larger. Did I look older in person? I didn't think so, but even if I did, his rudeness was unwarranted.

"I'm nineteen," I said lightly. Instead of apologizing or asking me what I meant, his nostrils flared. He spun on his heels and left.

I counted the extent of our exchange. How - one, *old -* two, *are -* three, *you -* four, *anyhow -* five. I was worth only five words to this man. *Was I that worthless?* I'd say my self-esteem was strong enough to withstand his insult. He was a nasty man, inside and out. What did I care what he said about me? He meant nothing to me. But my chin began to quiver and I could feel the tears come. Perhaps it was the shock of his behavior, the beauty of the evening, the scent of the roses, the music of the carousel nearby, the sorrow that I was not only alone, but alone in Bryant Park full of happy-go-lucky couples; that I had been dumped for my age or looks; that my situation was growing worse and worse; that I couldn't fall off a horse and climb back on again and again and again.

The tears flowed. I didn't want to cry in the park or in the subway, but I could not stop. I called a friend who worked nearby. I went there and cried and cried and cried till I couldn't cry anymore. He had said only five words, but I felt I had gone through a terrible ordeal that took me over an hour to get over. I was "stood up" in the cruelest way possible. Though I was left standing in the park while he walked off, I was not "standing" at all. I was "collapsing" under the weight of his cruelty. There was nothing "up" about this. It was all "down." I learned that "stood up" really means "collapse down."

Going into Shock

I met Shock online. He had not grown up religious, but after his divorce he had discovered his heritage, studied, and become religious. He had given me references. I didn't want a repeat of my last date. We met after work at a restaurant and I was a bit surprised by his appearance. On his online profile, he had been clean-shaven and wearing an argyle sweater. He appeared with a long shaggy beard, dressed in a black hat and suit – the uniform of the more right-wing yeshiva guy. He seemed to punctuate his language with *yeshivish* lingo: *Baruch Hashem* – Thank God, *Im Yirtzeh Hashem* – God willing. Nothing wrong with that, but it seemed a bit forced – as though he was trying to prove to me how religious he was.

Perhaps hearing that I was *frum* from birth had prompted all this? I felt like telling him he needn't try that hard. It was okay to be himself. I was sincere about *frumkeit*, but not particularly *yeshivish*. I liked the fact that he was a mix of worldly and *frum*.

We chitchatted and eventually I did remark on how different he looked online than in person. He admitted that he thought women would like him better if he played the part. I reassured him that he was fine just as he truly was.

On our second date, I was again surprised. Shock had shaved off his beard and dressed casually. He was really handsome without all that facial hair. I did feel more comfortable with this mode of dress, but something in his manner had changed too. He was unburdening himself and talking about how difficult it was to be divorced and alone

– totally not considering, as so many others hadn't, that throughout all the years he had been married, I had been alone.

I told him so.

Then Shock did the math. I could literally see his brain racing, calculating, thinking of something he had never thought of before today.

"Wait a second here, didn't you tell me you're *frum* from birth?" he asked. "Yes, I did," I nodded.

"And you haven't ever been married?"

"No."

"I cannot believe that. You seem so put together!" His brows furrowed. "So you've never…?" he was clearly too shocked to finish his thought.

"No I've never. Never," I said, knowing what he meant.

"Wow. You're still a virgin?" he was incredulous, but apparently had recovered enough to say what he was thinking. Though he himself just alluded to how difficult abstaining was, it hadn't occurred to him that anyone unmarried who was FFB would be a virgin. He was floored.

I nodded.

"Even my daughter is not a virgin anymore," he exclaimed.

Oh, the things people say! Now it was my turn to be shocked and do some mental calculations. *How old did he say his daughter was? Fifteen? Sixteen?* I knew he had not been religious and that his daughter was not. I knew the world out there had very different values, but I was not prepared to hear this. *Even if true, why would he share something so personal about his own child so soon? Was this a point of pride or shame for him?* I honestly couldn't tell. I was at a loss for words. So, he continued.

"We could get a hotel room right now and I'll show you what you've been missing!" He waved his arm towards the imaginary room somewhere in this vast city behind him. Yeshiva clothes and lingo were totally gone now. He was clearly agitated that I had missed out. This went way beyond asking whether I was *shomer negiah*, I thought.

As deprived or lonely as I felt, this wasn't the way it was going to happen. I was not accepting on-the-spot offers. Where was the righteous guy he was pretending to be last time? I wanted to be married properly *k'das Moshe v'Yisroel.* I wanted a proposal from someone I knew – not a proposition from someone I didn't. I was a *bas Yisrael* who wanted to behave as a proper Jew for God, despite all my slip-ups.

I went home and felt sorrow for the world, for myself, and for youngsters raised in a culture devoid of values, a culture where nothing was shocking any longer.

Arithmetic

I turned thirty-five and was still not married. This wasn't what I expected for myself, but this was the reality, so I continued to learn, grow, work, play, volunteer and, of course, husband-hunt. It was akin to job hunting. When there were no friends setting me up, no single events, nothing online, I'd review my list of matchmakers. I called one who had tried to help in the past.

"How old are you now?" she asked.

"Thirty-five," I said. It rankled me that age always appeared to be the primary factor.

"I have no one for you. Once you're thirty-five years old it's basically over." *Over? Like in standing-in-front-of-a-firing-squad over?*

"Men want younger women." Had she said she had no one she could think of now, that would be one thing, but that's not what she had said. She said it was over. *No one? So, is that it? Do I give up? What do you mean "no one?" What are you suggesting lady? That I join a convent? Jump off a roof?* I was horrified.

A day or two later, I got an email from a never-married bachelor who was fifty-five years old. *Oh, brother! What was HE thinking?* I normally ignored such people, but now that I was officially a non-entity at thirty-five, I wanted to get my two-cents in. I click-clacked that keyboard.

"Don't you think a twenty-year age gap is a bit much?" I typed.

"Not at all," he wrote back. "My rabbi said up to twenty years age difference is perfectly fine!" He seemed delighted that this "young" lady had indeed responded. I could imagine him planning our date, our marriage, our kids.

"Well, good luck on your next date with a seventy-five-year-old!" I hit return.

On another occasion, a blind date started the conversation as so many do about age. "So how old are you?"

"You're kind of putting me on the spot here. Didn't anyone tell you it's not polite to ask a woman that question? Why didn't you check with the matchmaker?"

"Oh, they all lie. I want you to tell me and I want you to be honest."

Honest. Every man who had ever lectured me about honesty had ended up being the most dishonest. Something in me snapped and I broke loose.

"Honest? You want me to be honest? When you tell me about your hairline, your waistline, your bottom line, your bank balance, your ex-wives, your criminal record, your height, your shoe size, your this and your that..." I was on an angry roll, "Then I might tell you my age!"

After he gathered his wits he said, "I think we're not compatible."

"No, we're not!"

It was getting more difficult to deal with age. I was watching younger and younger people get married. First it was just those who were a few grades younger, then it was kids I had babysat or had as campers. In my late thirties, some of my classmates who had married at a very young age were marrying off their kids at that tender age as well.

All this talk of age and fertility led me to inquire about freezing my eggs. When I first inquired, I was told the option was only available to women undergoing chemo. A few years later, when the process was more commonplace, I would ask again and be told that I had passed the age limit.

I was at a family bar mitzvah when a neighbor approached me and said she had a date for me. It was nice to have a random date come my way instead of me doing all the work. Then I heard a bit about the guy and was hesitant. He didn't appear to be what I was looking for. That's when the pressure was applied. The usual comments. "*You never know...*

God willing… Don't shoot yourself in the foot." I relented and agreed to let him call me. But instead, later that day, the neighbor pulled me aside.

"I just need to ask you something," she said.

"Yes?"

"I need to ask your age."

"I'm sorry, I don't feel comfortable revealing it," I said. "I can tell you what age range I'm looking for."

"You must tell me your age. I can't set you up if I don't know your age," she insisted.

"Other people do all the time. Surely you must have some ballpark idea if you thought of this gentleman for me?"

I had not asked for her help. She had insisted, and now this?

"Well, I need to know if you're fertile."

"Fertile?"

"Yes, fertile."

"Even twenty-year-olds don't know whether they're fertile and I don't know either. I've never tested out my equipment." I turned and walked away.

Ever since that *shadchan* told me it was "over," I really didn't feel comfortable revealing my age. I learned that whether or not I told the truth about my age, my response was never a good one. Men wanted women under thirty-five and they had their pick. If I told the truth, they assumed that everyone fudged their age, and that I was older than I truly was. Or they believed me and felt I was too old anyhow. If I lied, I felt like a fraud.

Turning thirty-five was the dawn of a lose-lose situation. I was learning that men who wanted children didn't want to meet me because they were afraid that I would be infertile, and men that didn't want more children did not want to meet me either because they were afraid that I wouldn't be.

Ageism had become a huge source of angst for me. Men would complain and state that they never lie about their age, but age was not a strike against a man. And, in fact, many men did lie. Sometimes it was glaring and obvious. I saw the liver spots, false teeth, wrinkles, or toupees. There was no way these men were the ages they claimed to be. But they could get dates with younger women, and with women their age, or even older. The main motive for a man to lie was to score a date with a woman much too young for him.

Men could make mistakes in their youth, redeem themselves as they matured, and still get a decent date at any age. Men were not beating a biological clock. They had the luxury of time as well as a vast pool of women to choose from.

Age was asked by every website, form, and matchmaker. But when I met men on my own, the first impression was my looks and personality. In my late thirties, I still looked much younger, which led to an interesting phenomenon. Blind date suggestions were all much older than me, while at parties, men who were way too young would ask me out.

At one weekend, I met a man that I did like, but I sensed our age difference. I asked around and found out he was indeed eleven years younger than me. I had dated younger men, but this age gap was too big for me. We were at different stages in our lives. Besides I believed that the minute he found out, he'd drop me.

I didn't want to tell him why I couldn't go out with him because then he'd know I was older and this issue was fraught with anxiety. I just told him we weren't a fit. He felt so rejected and hurt – not realizing the truth. So, there I was getting turned down by age-appropriate men and at the same time reluctantly rejecting men far more appealing because they were more than a decade younger. That period was a twilight zone.

To some, perhaps I had been an object, an idea, a symbol, a statistic more than a person. But now I'd been degraded to a number. What mattered was not the number I was, but the number I was not; the number I passed and could never return to. The age the man was, minus ten or minus fifteen. Or sometimes even plus eleven or minus twenty-five. It was the man's number that I had to be added to or subtracted from. I had liked arithmetic in school, but when it came to dating, I hated numbers.

Meant to Be

I was spending a week with a friend in Los Angeles. Friday night at our *Shabbos* dinner, I told her and her husband all the unusual places and times I had run into Singular. The guy had continually surprised me, in the playground, in Crown Heights, in restaurant windows, on Purim. Years had passed but we regularly ran into each other in the unlikeliest of places.

"Coincidence," said her husband. I was surprised because I expected him to believe that everything was Divine Providence.

During the ensuing years, we had run into each other at so many singles' events and crossed paths so often that I had grown very comfortable with Singular. I felt our *hashkafos*, intellectual curiosity, interests and personalities, meshed well but he never seemed to agree, despite clearly being fond of me. I supposed he had commitment issues.

"I disagree," I said to my friend's husband. "I think God keeps crossing our paths for a reason."

"It's coincidence, and you better move on," he repeated.

The next morning, my friend and I went to *shul*. I peeked through the *mechitzah* and felt goosebumps go up my arm.

"I think I see him," I whispered to my friend.

"Who?"

"Singular! That's the back of his neck!" *Could he really be here? Did we go on vacation to the same city, the same week, and attend the same shul?*

"That could be anybody's neck," she rolled her eyes. I tried to concentrate on my prayers, but I couldn't wait till *davening* was over. We all streamed to the *Kiddush* for wine and light fare. To my friend's amazement and my elation, Singular was indeed there. We exchanged pleasantries but, once again, he wasn't moved by the "coincidence" while I was certain – and now my friend was convinced, as well – that this was *Hashgachah Pratis*. This was meant to be.

"Would you like to do some sightseeing together this week?" I asked.

"Would've been happy to, but I'm leaving tomorrow to go see some

155

National Parks with my friends." I felt a twinge of regret. This could've been a good opportunity to reconnect. *Why would we meet in this fashion if nothing was to come of it?*

The next morning, I met a local man for brunch. It went well and somewhat assuaged my disappointment at Singular's departure.

Then came Monday.

My friend and I decided to spend the day sightseeing. We left at noon and traveled to a museum, only to discover it was not open on Mondays. So, we flipped through the dog-eared travel book to choose another destination. We drove in circles and could not find it. Our third destination was closed for renovations. And so, our afternoon passed. We drove and drove for hours and got nowhere. Finally, right before 5:00 pm, we wound up at the Los Angeles County Museum of Art in downtown LA. When we noticed that the museum was closing in minutes, we resigned ourselves to having wasted our day. We would go out for dinner and call it a day. As we walked back to our car, I spotted a sign for the sculpture garden near the museum.

"Why don't we check this garden out? It's free. At least we can feel as though we did *something* today." She agreed, so I charged down the deserted path, eager to see the sculptures. From a distance I spotted a hobo napping on a bench. I was ready to whiz right by him before my friend spotted him and u-turned for the exits. Then I noticed it wasn't a hobo after all. The man was dressed nicely and appeared to be resting with his arm draped over his face. The familiar goosebumps were back. *Could it be?*

I tiptoed gingerly to get closer and check. My shadow crossed his face. He awoke with a start. We both froze for a moment, then burst out with "What are you doing here?"

Singular sat up, ran his hand through his hair, smiled at me warmly, and asked again, "What are you doing here?"

"I'm sightseeing. The question is what are *you* doing here? Weren't you off to the National Parks? You told me you were leaving!"

He explained that his friend had been injured in a car accident, so he had spent the day with him in the hospital and the plans had changed. "Another friend," he pointed to the office building across the street, "is going to drive me to the bus station shortly – as soon as he gets out of work." It was 5:00 pm.

He had arrived early, found this garden, sat down and said some Psalms. He pulled his small *Tehillim* out of his pocket to show me. Then, worn out from the day's drama, he laid down to rest only moments earlier.

Only God could engineer this one.

I told him how my friend and I had driven all day to come to this one deserted spot in the entire city. *We had shown up moments after he had finished saying Tehillim. Does he see God's hand in any of this? Or would he resign this to "coincidence" once again?*

"Do you still think this is all just coincidence?" Aside from us three, the garden was entirely deserted.

He looked at me intently and said, "No, not this time. No."

"Can we talk about this when we return to NY?"

"Yes. Yes, we can. I'll call you."

We wished each other well. My heart thumped at this breakthrough. Finally. It was meant to be.

A number of weeks later, he still had not called. I was not sure how many days he was traveling; perhaps he was unsure about my plans as well. I was comfortable enough to call, and so I did.

"I was gonna call. I was gonna call. I was gonna call." He seemed overly apologetic. It seemed unnecessary. I was just glad we would finally talk.

"I was going to call before you heard from someone else." Heard what? Had someone passed?

"What are you talking about? What happened?"

"You mean you didn't hear?"

"Hear what?"

"That I'm engaged."

Surely, I heard wrong.

"I'm engaged," he repeated. I was shaken to my core and left speechless.

"You there?" he asked.

"Uh-huh." My mind couldn't make sense of this – I was trying to squeeze a square into a circle.

"I... I met her before LA, and then when I returned, we dated some more. And I'm engaged."

I couldn't think of what to say. I couldn't even think. I had thought we were "meant to be" in every way.

"You are intelligent and nice and..." *Oh spare me. I don't want to hear this speech again – the one where they tell you how wonderful you are but they prefer to marry someone else. I can't hear this.* I was trembling, but I let him say what he had to – all the wrong words.

Then I too, said what I had to. "Mazel tov. I wish you well." What else could I say? He was a good person. He deserved happiness. I didn't understand it.

In some metaphysical dimension, I felt a door whoosh close. It slammed shut. I shivered. I felt bereft in a way I had not ever felt before. This didn't feel like the other rejections. This felt like fate gone awry. What had years of Divine Providence led to? What had it all meant? Would I ever find out? How did free will work in concert with Divine Providence? Can free will change or subvert Providence? Had he ever, in any way, been my *basherte*? Was it all my imagination? He would marry someone else, so that must be God's will.

But I could not shake the feeling that I had lost the one that was meant to be.

Kabbalist

I rode the elevator up and walked past the peeling paint walls to the kabbalist's office. Perhaps it was that metaphysical door whoosh or the feeling of fate gone awry that finally led me here. It was an old apartment building and didn't seem like the right setting for a man who could see things I could not. I'm not sure what I was expecting – perhaps a yeshiva or synagogue stacked high with holy books or a Rabbi Shimon Bar Yochai-type cave in a secret garden. This hallway was too ordinary.

The walls were a faded mint green. A non-Jewish man scurried past me to catch the elevator before it went down again.

The office door was shut and there was an apologetic, hand-scribbled note taped to the door stating an emergency had come up and that all appointments would have to be rescheduled. I had rushed over from the subway station, my hair and clothes were plastered to me, and I was still panting. The skeptic in me grew more skeptical. If this kabbalist can see into the future, couldn't he have foreseen his emergency far enough in advance to call and alert his clients?

Who was this man? Why was I pinning any hopes on him anyway? I had heard about him through the grapevine. Several Sephardic Jews deeply into mysticism and kabbalists had mentioned this rabbi's name to me. They had told me he could suggest *segulos* – actions that can lead to a change in one's destiny for the better. This man "knew stuff," they said emphatically, without telling me much more. "Just go and see for yourself." *What did he know? One's past? Could he read minds? Predict the future? What* segulos *would he suggest to me? Was he truly a* mekubal?

I recalled other *brachos* I had received and *segulos* I had tried with mixed results. Their efficacy would indeed miraculously yield date suggestions after a long dry spell – but one man never called, the other lived on the other side of the world with no plans to travel, and a third turned out to be an alleged child molester. *What was the point?*

I wasn't sure if the fee went to a charity or directly to him, but I would chalk it up to charity. Many people had told me about this *mekubal*. I felt compelled to try everything I could, at least once. I knew I'd return despite my doubts.

When the subway delayed me for my rescheduled appointment with him, I didn't bother racing over or sweating it out. I arrived a few minutes late. This time the door was ajar and I was startled to see a bustling crowd in the waiting area. It was more crowded than a doctor's office. I was astounded. A short, bearded assistant shoved a clipboard at me and asked me to sign it and wait my turn. The air was stifling, a fan whirred lazily and ineffectively.

But the people buzzed with excitement.

159

"*This* mekubal *is fantastic. I come here every week,*" one woman said.

"*He told me to check my* mezuzah. *When I came home, it had fallen off the doorpost. Isn't it amazing that he knew?*"

"*My sister followed his directions and was engaged only two weeks later!*"

I calculated that were I to meet someone right here, right now, in the waiting room, I would nevertheless not be engaged in two weeks. It would take a miracle and a bit of insanity on my part for that to happen. The likelihood was very close to zero, *mekubal* or no *mekubal*.

My spirit was soaring and diving as I did not know what to think. I very much wanted to believe this was the last pitstop on my road to marriage. When I admitted my skepticism to the woman sitting next to me, she chided me. "You must have *emunah* – faith – and follow his instructions. If you are skeptical, it will not work." Implying that if nothing changed for me, it would be no one's fault but my own.

This bothered me greatly. Because I did have faith, but I had faith in God, not a *mekubal* in a stuffy little apartment in Brooklyn.

God is All-Knowing and Almighty. If making matches was as hard as splitting the Red Sea, He alone could make it happen. What could this mekubal *possibly tell me that would change my fate, split my sea, allow me to escape my Egypt?*

Two hours and two sweaty armpits later, I found out. I entered his office stuffed with holy books and to my surprise, the *mekubal* looked as though he had not passed his fortieth birthday yet – the age when one is permitted to study kabbalah. He looked very young. *Had he studied all these books?* I was afraid to let doubts cloud my thinking in case he could read my mind. I just wanted help getting married.

I tried to blank my mind. *Blank. Blank. Blank. Wipe that slate clean. Erase it.* He told me several things about myself. Some of it he got right, and some of it he got very, very wrong. I was worried. *Could it be he knew things about me that I didn't know? Was he a psychic or a fake? Blank, blank, blank. Swipe, wipe, erase.*

I got right to the point, "Am I getting married this year?" *This year.*

I wanted to know. Not "yes, some time…maybe soon…future." This year is what I wanted to hear.

"You're hard to read," he said. *No wonder! I had just mentally swiped and wiped.* My slate was pure white now.

"You're surrounded by a black cloud," he continued. "I can't see a thing." In one moment, my white slate had been replaced by a black cloud.

"A black cloud? What do you mean?" I asked.

"You have a very bad *ayin hora* – evil eye – blocking you. Perhaps people are envious of you?"

He gave me a list of prayers to say – forty-five minutes' worth – and told me the most auspicious time to say them was the time King David had prayed – in the middle of the night. I was to do it for seven weeks to pierce the black clouds. I gave him my *mezuzah* scrolls they had told me to bring in for him to check. I didn't think they were damaged, as I'd had them checked recently by a professional scribe.

I was dejected. Everyone else in the waiting room seemed to merit miracle stories, but I was black-clouded and hustling for favors from God. But I was resolved to give it my all. At least this once. Again.

For the next seven weeks, I went to bed earlier, set my alarm, woke up in the middle of the night, and prayed with more focus and energy than I had thought possible at that hour. I really did feel alone with God at that hour. I spoke to Him and cried to Him as I imagined King David had. Then I crawled back into bed, confident He would diffuse the black cloud around me.

At my next visit, I waited expectantly, despite my initial skepticism. Those weeks of self-discipline and intense nightly prayer had infused me with strong hope. *This is it. I will get good news and good fortune.* I waited and sweated once again. He told me my cloud was now gray. *Gray? All that davening and I had merely shifted from black to gray? Was my skepticism the problem? Or were all those people being fooled?* I didn't know. I asked whether he had checked my *mezuzah.* He was sorry, but my *mezuzah* scroll had been misplaced.

I never went back.

The Big Four-O

My fortieth birthday was just around the corner and it was terrifying in so many ways, as superficial milestones often are. Why forty should be so much more terrifying than thirty-nine was illogical. I would still only be a year older than the year before, but it felt as though I was skipping an entire decade. Getting a date (and getting pregnant after marriage) would be exponentially more difficult. And I was still mourning Singular.

Time marched on. I attended *shiurim* which filled me with faith and hope and assuaged my worries. That lasted until I once again lay in a sorrowful, spent heap, clutching my blankets in the dark of night after another woeful date.

I would need to be more selective about my dates. If the gentleman was nice, but not for me, I would at least have a pleasant evening and remain upbeat about my future prospects. But when my dates were humiliating, they discouraged me and chipped away at my optimism. The volume of unsuitable dates was beginning to wear on my self-esteem. They made me question my own worth.

I didn't walk around wearing my sorrow on my sleeve. I tried to smell the roses along the way and appreciate the cup half full rather than half empty. I was asked, "How can you be so happy if you're single?" *Would they rather see me bitter and unhinged? What is wrong with people?* They obviously weren't there when the tears were flowing or when I was letting off steam. My family faced the brunt of my despair. My mother's shoulders sagged with the weight of my tears. I snapped at or whined to my siblings for having botched any potential *shidduch* attempts. I always worked on tamping down jealousy at others' good fortune, but it was not easy.

As for God, I wrestled with Him most. On good days, I tried to improve, do more *chesed*, give more charity, be careful with *lashon hara*, say more *Tehillim*, be a better Jew. I prayed to Him, begged Him, tried to make deals with Him. On the bad days, in my despair, I threatened

Him – *I'll run off with a gentile if You don't help me marry before forty* – as though I had the power to challenge Him.

It's human nature to compare ourselves to those better off than we are, rather than to millions around the world less fortunate. In many respects, I knew I was far more fortunate than others, but it's not easy to keep things in perspective all the time.

Regarding solitude, I was blessed to be alone outside of a marriage rather than alone inside of one. I was safe and healthy when others were abused or endangered by their spouses. I knew marriage was not a fairy tale and that people have a slew of other problems within them – problems that would not burden me. But still. I was tired of being alone.

I was often invited by others or hosted my own guests. Yet, there were Shabbosim or Yomim Tovim on my own. I was weary of being a third wheel, a guest or a spouseless hostess. I didn't always feel like asking around for meal invites. I was tired of walking home late at night on my own, or packing an overnight bag, traveling, and sleeping in someone else's spare room. And while I usually had no trouble with peace or solitude, after a loud, crowded, joyous occasion elsewhere, mists of loneliness would seep in when I returned to my quiet, empty apartment.

Now, heading towards the Big 4-0, I felt lost, lonely, and scared.

I marveled at how others married several times while I couldn't manage it even once. How did widowers remarry weeks after losing a spouse? Were they taking reckless leaps of faith? Was I overthinking things? Combining mature lives with a load of baggage is so much more overwhelming than young love. I couldn't dive in blindly.

There were women who made it their goal to marry before the Big 4-0, at any cost. They married men who had not given their previous spouse a *get*, men who had been jailed for crimes, men who had abandoned their own children or men who argued, lied, or belittled them in public. I was desperate, but not *that* desperate. What could compel these women to make those dreadful choices? Was it abject loneliness, status, financial security, maternal instinct? I don't know,

163

but for me, anyone with serious negative behaviors was not remotely suitable as a match. Were the decent men all married? Were those recently widowed or divorced bombarded with long lists of women?

What would happen if I reached out to *anyone* interested in meeting an Orthodox Jewish woman? Anyone. I just wanted to meet a decent man I could talk to. I was aching for it. So, on the eve of my fortieth birthday, when I felt estranged from God and anyone connected with my dating life, I decided to cast a wider net and see what would happen. I did it for a lark. I did it to shake things up. I did it to rattle God. I did it because "you never know." I did it because I was feeling reckless, humiliated, petty, childish, pained, and despairing.

If I was entering a new decade, I would do so with a bang. I clicked away on my computer, hit return, then I went to sleep on my last night as a thirty-nine-year-old. Tomorrow I'd wake up to the Big 4-0.

GothGuy

I woke up feeling very much the same. I hadn't aged a decade overnight. I was still despondent, but had given myself something artificial to look forward to. I thought of my inbox as a stack of glittering birthday presents to unwrap. First, I would say my morning prayers. I had not given up on God but felt, rightly or wrongly, that God had given up on me. I was still hoping against hope He'd grant me a miracle as a last-minute birthday gift. I knew there was very little chance someone Jewish would write to me. If that should happen, it was highly unlikely we would hit it off, and even less probable that this person would be interested in a religious way of life. If God would grant me a miracle, it would happen through normal channels, not some random website. I knew my prayers and faith were not consistent. I prayed to God to see inside my heart and know my intentions were honorable, even when I seemed to waver. This was a coping strategy at passing yet another birthday as a single woman.

I clicked on my inbox and, to my delight, found a few dozen emails. My Pavlovian chemical reaction triggered a release of dopamine – the "reward" neurotransmitter, serotonin the chemical that makes one feel valued, and endorphins that provide excitement. This was exactly the kind of feel-good distraction I needed. It was this or a tub of Neapolitan ice cream. My inbox had zero calories. I was psyched.

One by one, as I clicked open the emails, my excitement quickly faded to disappointment. The foul language and indecent suggestions burst my bubble very fast. *Oh well, what did I expect? It was a really stupid idea.* I was once again feeling sorry for myself. I had a few emails left. Click. Trashed. Click. Trashed. Click. *Oh.*

Oh.

And there was GothGuy. He looked like a goth rock star, dressed in black, masculine, but his wild, dark long hair gave him a bit of an androgynous pretty-as-a-girl look. He wasn't remotely like anyone I knew. His email was polite, friendly, and curious. I knew we were as different as night and day. He was not Jewish, not remotely what I was looking for, and definitely never would be. I was curious to see why he would write to an Orthodox woman. He claimed he had many Jewish friends. I assumed none of them were Sabbath observant.

God alone knows why I agreed to meet him. For the same reasons I clicked that keyboard in the first place. A lark. Nothing better going on. Anger. We met, and he could barely look me in the eye. He stuttered and bragged and seemed nervous. Was I intimidating? I didn't think so. Was I as unexpected for him as he was for me? For my part, I was very uncomfortable to be seen with him. He was dressed in black, head to toe.

Through my work experience I had learned that one could not judge a person by his clothing. Some people in formal business attire used foul language and were very crass people. While others with piercings, purple hair, and tie-dye shirts were respectful of my religious convictions.

He was courteous and pleasant, but all I could think of was *What am I doing here? What was I thinking? Let me just get through this and go home.* I was mortified to be seen socially with someone like him outside of a business setting.

"I have a lot of Jewish friends," he said as though that made him an expert on Judaism. I knew he probably had no idea what observance was. I had met non-Jews before who had a very rudimentary understanding of Judaism. They simplified Bar Mitzvahs as some kind of birthday party or joked about how it was their favorite "bar." Eating kosher was reduced to not eating pork and Yom Kippur was merely a day of fasting, but that was all they knew. They really weren't aware of the intricacies of Jewish law or the depth of observance. It was true of GothGuy as well. I could tell that we were from different galaxies, but he didn't see it at all. He was very chatty and friendly. Though I was dressed more modestly than the women he knew, I didn't look as alien to him as the Chassidim who scurried by him in the street with no eye contact.

"What is it with those guys? They don't even *walk* like the rest of us," he said. I felt indignant on their behalf because I understood their lifestyle.

That religious world was foreign and strange to him. He didn't believe in God and was convinced that religious sects were all outdated cults.

I felt like I was viewing him through a one-way mirror. I lived as a Jew within his society. I understood how different my life was from the surrounding culture. I had seen it via the schoolyard and neighborhood, mainstream media, college, and my jobs in corporate America. He had no concept of my relationship to *Hashem* or my sense of Judaism's mission, purpose, and centrality to world events. He could not fathom why anyone would willingly cling to tradition. He was sure religious men treated their wives horribly. He acted as though I were trapped against my will. He would help liberate me from all that nonsense. The more comments he made to that effect, the more irritated I became. I had heard all this before from others. The more he talked, the more meeting him felt like a huge mistake.

We parted and I went home relieved that it was over and amazed at my ability to do stupid things again and again. What had compelled me to write on that website or to agree to meet him? I must have been out of my mind. That was just it. I *was* out of my mind. I was perpetually *the* single one at family events. I was lonely. I had normal drives that were not being met. I was deprived 365 days a year in ways others were deprived only on Yom Kippur or during a week of *shiva*. Being single was a constant cycle of hope, rejection, and despair. I was constantly peeling myself up off the ground to start over, with the spiritual stamina of a champion heavyweight lifter. It was brutal.

Ping. Another email from him. His flirtatious nature was light and humorous – not threatening at all. Even though I was appalled that I had met him, he was apparently delighted to have met me. I could feel the dopamine, serotonin and endorphins race through my neurons against my will, like a pinball lighting up bumpers as it zigzagged through the playfield. I was not used to this positive attention at all.

He was different all right. For one thing, I was smart enough to know his motivations were different than those of my blind dates. They were cutting to the chase, sometimes too quickly, trying to pin down if I met their criteria. Beauty? Check. Parents? Check. Job? Check? I often felt interviewed for a position as Wife, while GothGuy was simply socializing and talking to me, trying to win me over with his charm. I knew he was trouble.

He didn't need to know where my father *davened*, or how many siblings I had, nor where they lived, or any of the other stale questions I was asked *ad nauseam*. Even though he wasn't what I was looking for or wanted, he was most definitely interesting, and he had a safe charm and sense of humor. He piqued my curiosity and injected some shine to the dullness around me. He was awakening me from my deep dating torpor. I clicked back. And so, the emails clicked back and forth. Talking with him, I didn't feel "single," "*nebechdik*", "over-the-hill," or rejected. I didn't exactly feel normal, and I was definitely playing with fire, but I felt human again.

I wondered. How does a man who looks this way live? Does he live in a normal apartment with a flowered couch, a dining room set, and venetian blinds? Or are his walls painted cave black? He told me he had two roommates and one was a female. In my world, that would never be acceptable, but it was a non-issue in his. And frankly, I was glad he had a female roommate because I was very curious about his home. Having a female there would make it possible to visit. I wasn't allowed to be alone with him for one thing and I barely knew him, so it certainly made a visit feel less risky.

They say curiosity killed the cat, but they also say a cat has nine lives. It was a foolish thing to do, but I didn't feel threatened at all. I had felt more fear on some of my *shidduch* dates. GothGuy was a very far cry from my world and our values and beliefs differed greatly, but he was a decent person. I was always an adventurous soul, curious about the world, other cultures and people's lives, so I went to see where he lived in Chinatown. He told me he had been stopped once in front of Mesivta Tifereth Yerushalayim on Shabbos and had been asked to flip a switch.

"Would God strike them dead if they did it themselves? I don't get it."

"Wow. You were a *Shabbos goy*?"

"Oy. Oy. I was a *Shabbos goy*," he sang in his sing-song manner. "Does that qualify me now?"

"Um, no. But you are funny. It's nice that you did it. Did you know Elvis was one too?"

We climbed up a rickety, narrow set of stairs and when he swung open the door all I saw was color. Purples and golds and reds and oranges. The walls were covered in posters, hangings, and masks painted in different shades of color.

"Oh wow, this feels more like a gallery than a home."

"My roommate did all of it, kiddo," he said, just as she came out through beaded curtains to greet me. There was a blur of fur and barks.

"You didn't tell me you have dogs," I said. A large mutt sniffed me lazily but the miniature greyhound barked and lunged at me.

"That's because they're not mine, kiddo. These belong to my roommate. I never understood why religious Jews are so nervous around dogs." I explained that some observant Jews did have pets, but many do not have any familiarity with animals, so it creates fear. Also, Holocaust survivors had often witnessed German Shepherds shred people to pieces. Some survivors had dog nightmares fifty years later. Yet my father wasn't afraid at all and used to call out for our neighbor's German Shepherd, "Hello, Princess!"

Many of our conversations drew on our different life experiences, which was interesting, but the "kiddo" thing annoyed me. At least he didn't view me as an old lady, and I did feel young around him, compared to my dates who made me feel over the hill. But I was no child. I was a forty-year-old woman! I could sense he thought I was incredibly sheltered and brainwashed.

I watched myself as though on a movie screen. I trusted myself, but if I were my own daughter, I would be horrified seeing her play with fire this way. I remembered the seventh-grade lesson about Yochanan Kohen Gadol. I was crossing lines here.

I was angry at God, but still talked to Him all the time. I was not denying His existence. I was acutely aware that He was watching the same movie starring "me." I was also aware that I had been begging to do the right thing for twenty years – to meet my mate and build a Jewish home. *Why hadn't it happened?* Yet my empty threat of running off with a gentile when I turned forty seemed to be what God heard, when one magically materialized *exactly* on my deadline. *Hashgachah Pratis.*

Was it a self-fulfilling prophecy? Should I have said confidently "I'll be a Jewish wife and mom by the time I'm forty" over and over? Instead of threatening God about what I'd do if I wasn't? Was God calling my bluff? Testing me? My head was spinning.

Live and Learn

I was aware of Jewish history and what generations of Christians and Muslims had inflicted on the Jews. There had been cycles of violence and peace. My father's friendly gentile neighbors had turned into looters and sneering enemies when he returned to his village. My mother's neighbor – the town police chief – had no qualms arresting her young cousin in the street for being a Jew without papers, though he knew exactly who he was.

I was also acutely aware that my parents were alive, thanks to the unfathomable risks and generosity of their non-Jewish rescuers. I knew how my mother's schoolteachers cried with joy and relief when my mother returned after the war alive and well. I knew we were all created in the image of God and some of us – Jew and non-Jew – rose to the occasion, and some of us failed miserably. I knew that as a Jew I had the blessing of the Torah's laws to guide me in the direction of good, coupled with the bonus mission of being a "light unto the nations."

I learned a lot in GothGuy's place. I learned that much of what I'd been taught was true. The Torah truly understands human nature and its laws are designed to protect us from harming ourselves. I've learned that we are all guilty of judging others and rationalizing ourselves, but ideally, we should judge ourselves and rationalize others. I learned that only we know our own motivations – and that sometimes we don't. And we can't possibly guess at those of others. I learned that I couldn't ignore God. I learned that regret brings one closer to God than ever.

I learned that my physical desires and my spiritual desires were at odds with each other. I learned that I could only unify and gratify those two conflicting desires modestly within a marriage sanctified by God and Israel. I learned that, faced with a choice, ultimately, I chose my spiritual desires over physical desires. There were lines I wouldn't cross. I wanted to do the right thing despite everything. I learned that humans fail, but God gives us ample opportunity to repent and be forgiven.

GothGuy was convinced my resistance to him was because I was afraid of my parents, but that's because he was an atheist. "It's your parents, kiddo, isn't it?"

"No, that's not it," I corrected him. "For one thing, I'm a grown woman and I have my own place. My parents wouldn't approve, but they're not here and would never know – unless you would tell them. But God *is* here, and He knows."

He rolled his eyes in disbelief and sighed. He believed morals came from common sense. But if that were the case, I argued through my tears, how could he explain a world full of violence, murder, theft, war, abuse, corruption, child trafficking, cannibalism and more? How did worldwide common sense disappear? Common sense was very subjective. There had to be an objective, moral standard from a Higher Authority. He sighed again.

There had been a few religious men across the observance spectrum who had made untoward passes at me or tried to. However most religious men did behave in that regard, and to his credit, when I made my boundaries clear, GothGuy did too. He may have thought it was his common sense that held him back, but he had grown up in a home with parents who instilled a Judeo-Christian foundation to his beliefs, despite his rejection of their church. That foundation had molded his "common sense" more than he realized. From that encounter, I learned I was very lucky. I had lived and I had learned, and God had been with me.

While we both moved on to date people more appropriate for each of us, he remained a loyal, supportive friend with no ulterior motives. We stayed in our lanes, guarded our boundaries, and though unconventional – and still as different from each other as can be – he became a truer friend to me than many others.

Attitude!

The next years were more of the same. Well almost. There were men who showed up hours late; who couldn't converse or meet my eye; who had awful secrets, criminal records, or no divorce; and those who were only interested in one thing. I had fewer and fewer options, and nothing was working out. But just when I thought I'd seen it all, there was always a new kind of crazy. At this point, I felt my experiences added up to an unexpected (and unwanted) master's degree in anthropological studies.

I sat next to Chubby at a Friday night singles' meal. I don't particularly care for chubby men, but he was so pleasant and easy to talk to that his weight took a backseat to his character. I really wanted to get to know him better. I asked our hostess later about him and was elated to hear that he had already inquired about me. She gave him my number and again, like many men before him, he failed to call. But I didn't give up. I called the hostess again and urged her to call him.

"Yes, he really likes you and is eager to call," she relayed his message. *Something was wrong. If he was eager to call, why hadn't he?* But then a few days later he did call! We had another very pleasant talk and then he said he had to go and would call me again. We hung up. *Why hadn't he asked me out?* Once again, I was left scratching my head.

When he called the following week, we had another nice talk, and again he said he had to go. I asked him if he'd like to meet. I really didn't want to have to do the asking, but he wasn't doing it for me. That's when the excuses began. *It looks like it's going to snow; I have a wedding Tuesday night; I go learn on Thursdays,* and on and on. I was disappointed, but Chubby seemed bright, interested in me, we had pleasant talks, and overall, he seemed to be a busy guy. He seemed worth the wait.

In time, a friend announced her engagement. She had kept her dating quiet, so it was a real surprise. When I asked her when she had met her *chosson*, she said they had met four months earlier. She had met him the very same week I had met Chubby! That's when the ridiculousness of my situation hit me with full force. *What was I doing? Four months had passed and we hadn't even gone on a single date! My friend had a whole relationship in the same time period and had gotten engaged. This was definitely a new kind of crazy. How had I allowed this to happen?* I was crestfallen. I had been a fool.

Chubby called again, "Hi, how are you?" he said in his upbeat manner.

"Well, there's something I need to ask you."

"Sure."

In as neutral and calm a voice as I could muster, I asked, "Do you or do you not want to go out with me?"

I could hear my heart thump.

Then.

"Well, if that's your attitude, forget it," he said.

He hung up.

My friend got married. As for me, I still had no date. I had attitude.

Black Hat

Throughout my years of dating, a pattern emerged. I found that the men that I connected with best religiously, socially, and intellectually were modern *baalei teshuvah*. They had grown up in a secular family and had either been sent to yeshiva or had become religious later on in life. They embraced the world and took religion seriously as well. I felt more comfortable with my own religious struggles in their presence. It was the combination most suited for me. I met plenty of men closer to my own demographic – Brooklyn child of Holocaust survivors – or *frum* from birth, and yet I never found common ground with them. When a colleague mentioned a Lakewood black-hat yeshiva guy, I didn't think the match was for me. I wrote it off as too far to the right for me.

Then someone else mentioned this same man, and then a third person. They all claimed he was exceedingly nice. I couldn't understand why a nice guy who had studied in the Lakewood Yeshiva Beth Medrash Govoha would still be single in his forties. *Don't they all marry at 20? What could be wrong with him?* Unfortunately, by this time, my past experiences had made me wary of *yeshivish* men, especially when things didn't add up. Moreover, I wasn't sure he'd agree to meet me. Wouldn't he prefer someone more *yeshivish?* All three contacts guaranteed me that he was a mensch and that I would not come home in tears. So, I relented, and to my surprise, he called. It would be my first "black hat" date in years.

Blackhat was a mensch. I was pleasantly surprised that everything the matchmakers told me was true this time. In his case, his years of Torah study *were* reflected in his behavior. He *was* polite, on time, generous, friendly and talkative. We went out for dinner and had a very relaxed meal. He seemed serious about marriage, so I couldn't believe he wasn't married yet. He told me he frequently traveled overseas for work. I sensed our different lifestyles, but I felt he was a good person.

I thought of how I griped to my mother after a long span of bad dates. I'd tell her that if only most of my dates were good, eligible men and all I had to do was find a compatible one, things would be easier to bear. However, as I got older, I often felt that I was dating so many men who weren't eligible for marriage at all. I had to find one man who was. Blackhat fit that bill. I felt we weren't a match, but he was good "husband material." If he wanted another date, I would go out with him again. I would not brush him aside so easily. I would definitely try. I could hear all the voices from years of unsolicited advice echoing in my mind, *Compatibility, comshmatibility doesn't matter... all you really need is a good person... You'll never find someone perfect...*

I was out with Blackhat on our second date. I wanted it to work despite our different observance levels and lifestyles. Could we make it work?

"You're the most normal woman I've gone out with in a very long time," he said.

"I can say the same about you. Well, I mean … most normal man," I said. "I dislike using that word but so many people are just not... normal."

"Yes… I agree so many are not. But do you get the same feeling I get about us?" he asked.

"I think so… I'm not certain what you're thinking," I said.

"I'm thinking that here I am with a smart, nice, pretty woman who I wish could be the one, but I just know is not. We're too different, aren't we? This feels all wrong."

It was a shame, and although others wouldn't understand, I knew exactly what he meant. We wished each other well, promised to keep each other in our prayers, and hoped we'd both meet the right one for us.

I tried to think of who I might know for him, but all my *yeshivish* friends were already married. I later heard that Blackhat married the woman he dated right after me. I was truly happy for him. I was also amazed. There were quite a few occasions where I had turned out to be the penultimate woman – the woman before the wife. Was it merely circumstance, or was it something I gave them? One man had, in fact, told me that he learned to be himself from me, which helped him marry the next woman. In most cases, it was probably mostly circumstance, but it happened often enough for me to notice.

I'd like to think that we do meet everyone for a reason. That we do learn from each other. For me, meeting Blackhat helped heal the decades-old damage that YeshivaGuy had wrought years ago. Blackhat helped me by being the epitome of a *yeshivish* mensch.

The Softest Shoulder

I wanted so much to walk down the aisle to the *chuppah* leaning on my parents' arms, especially my mother's. She was my bedrock throughout my life, especially when it came to all the heartache in husband-hunting. Hers was the softest shoulder. My father wanted to see me married, but my mother felt my pain. She let me cry my heart out. She patted and soothed me. She told me my time would come. She heard my stories. Surely, I weighed her down with my tears. I felt guilty knowing that she had lost her mother at a tender age and here I was, an adult, still sobbing on her shoulders like a child. She assured me that her job had no retirement age.

When I moved out, I didn't always share my stories. I didn't want to give her false hope or disappoint her when prospects did not work out. As she got older, her health issues multiplied, and as my wedding date seemed as elusive as ever, I tried to face reality. I was able to have difficult conversations with my mother.

"What if after 120 years, I'm not married yet and you're gone? Do you think you could shake the heavens for me and make something happen up there?"

"If it's possible, of course," she said. Both of us hoped it wouldn't come to that.

"If I do marry afterwards, I would want you to know who I married. Could you come to me in a dream and let me know that you know?" Perhaps I did not have enough *emunah* or was acting like a fool, but these questions truly tugged at me. The person who most deserved to see me married was my mother.

Then one day a dreaded call came, and the unthinkable began – the hospitals, doctors, tests, charts, and the suffering. I watched my father suffer as he watched my mother suffer. Watched my mother suffer and suffer. We watched and worried and felt so helpless while trying to find some way to save her life. We experienced a fraction of all the worrying my parents had spent their lifetimes worrying over their children. Till one day we started praying to God to take her out of her agony. We questioned, prayed, waited, and watched. One day, we kissed our unresponsive mother. We leaned over and whispered, "We'll be okay. If you need to go, then go." We sang to her and watched her blood pressure rise and fall with our voices. Then she was gone. Even when expected, when the time arrived, the moment was utterly surreal and earth-shaking.

Family dynamics shift, reality changes, the anchor of our family was gone. Loss accentuates one's own mortality. All my fears that had been pushed beneath the surface bubbled up. My biological clock was ticking. What if I never had children? Who would care for me in my old age? Who would say *kaddish* for me? Who would miss me, the way a child misses its mother?

During *shiva*, some people put their foot in their mouth, as I'm sure I've done at times myself. As the only unmarried sibling, they felt it necessary to lament that my mother "never had *nachas*" from me. In the evening, after the *shiva* callers left, I unburdened myself to my family. I knew people fished for what to say, but the comment wounded me.

My father who had always left the job of consoler-in-chief to my mother, uncharacteristically took up her mantle and replied, "It takes no talent or genius to get married or have kids. It's *mazel*. God arranges matches. But it takes plenty of talent and genius to…" and he listed all the things I had done that gave him and my mother *nachas*. My eyes misted. I knew I had given my mother plenty of *nachas* in other ways, but still – she would not walk me down the aisle at my wedding. My mother – my softest shoulder.

Back and the JeanStalk

During my mother's illness I had no time or head for dating. After her passing, I had no desire. I grieved for months, and then one day I felt ready to begin again. I hoped my mother would be a heavenly advocate for me. She would shake the heavens for me if she could.

A neighbor set me up with Back. She told me that Back seemed like a nice guy. I researched a bit and heard that Back's divorce had been acrimonious. I would keep that in mind if there were any red flags. I was a bit wary of being his first date after his divorce, as he had gotten married very young. Sure enough, although he was in his fifties, I would only be the fifth woman he had ever dated in his lifetime.

It could've been refreshing to be with someone for whom dating was a new adventure rather than men who were completely jaded, but it wasn't. I felt I had reverted back to my early dating years of nervous formal dates.

We walked along the East River and stuck out noticeably; he wore his Shabbos suit and hat, while others biked or strolled in jeans and t-shirts. I preferred the anonymity of casual business attire in a kosher restaurant or a fun activity. I never felt at ease in a public space with the formality that announced, "here is an Orthodox couple on a blind date."

We had been walking a while when he suggested dinner. I consented. The meal was okay too, with the usual small talk. I wasn't feeling strongly either way about him, which was fine for a first date. When dinner was over, he suggested a nightclub. I was not interested. For one thing, we had already spent several hours together. It was our first date and it took time for me to warm up to people. I had no desire to jam in as much as I could on a first date. More importantly, I was still an *avel* and could not attend a live music venue.

"I think the walk and dinner were enough for me for a first date," I said as politely as I could. I was not rejecting him, I just had enough for the evening. But he seemed floored. He had not expected that. He was clearly enamored with me, surprised that I didn't feel the same.

"The time has flown by! It felt very brief!" he exclaimed.

"It's actually been more than three hours. That's longer than many of my first dates," I pointed out.

"My ex and I went on a nine-hour date for our first date," he persisted. *Right, and how did that work out? She's your ex now, isn't she?* I didn't voice what I thought but I felt like he was pushing it.

"Well, everyone's different. Anyhow no clubs for me. I'm an *avel*," I said, glad to have an airtight excuse. He took me home which gave us *another* hour of talk. Back made it apparent that he was very reluctant to end the date. He was beginning to grate on my nerves.

Before dropping me off, he asked me out again. When I want to be asked out again, of course I don't mind, but when I'm uncertain and want to think about it, I wish they'd go back to the person who set us up instead of putting me on the spot. His persistence and adulation had worn me out. I needed space to clear my head and think this through. I was slightly irritated but had no good reason to decline. Yet I was not feeling eager either. I told him the truth.

"I really want to give this some thought. I'll let my neighbor know how I feel and she'll get back to you," I said. He took it as a punch to his gut, a dagger to his heart – as though a long relationship had just ended.

"Oh, you don't want another date! I can't believe it. We were getting along so well!"

"I didn't say I don't want another date. I said I want to think about it."

"You're just being polite because you don't know how to say 'no,'" he countered. The one upside of a blind date is having an intermediary, especially if one is unsure of the answer. But this guy was sure he had all the answers, and now we had a problem.

"Actually, you're wrong. I do want to think about it, but the way you're acting right now is making this decision easier."

"Ok, ok, I'm sorry. Take as much time as you need. I'll wait to hear back," he said. "But really what is there to think about? You either want another date or you don't."

He was turning me off. We said our goodnights and I closed the door behind me feeling mentally exhausted. I would call my neighbor this week and talk it over with her.

I had not even settled in yet when my phone rang. It was my neighbor. Back must've called her while still parked outside my home. It was unsettling. I couldn't relax, put the evening aside, and think it through later. It was forcibly back in my conscience.

"He is very interested and would like to see you again," she said.

"We literally just ended our date moments ago and it all felt so formal. I told him I need time to think it over and that I would get in touch with you within the week. I can't believe he called you so soon."

"Yes, he's a bit persistent. He said if you can't decide tonight then he won't go out with you." *He's giving me an ultimatum? Then I'm done.*

"Ok, I decided. I'm not going out with him. He's too pushy," I said. She agreed that Back needed to back off, and apologized for passing on the message. She said she would try to talk some sense back into him. Thing is, I was losing any bit of interest I may have had. I felt more drained than ever.

The phone rang again. I assumed it would be her, but it wasn't. He was Back. Again. I could not believe it. He talked non-stop for forty-five minutes, apologizing for his earlier behavior. He was oblivious to his current behavior. I pulled the phone away from my ear. It didn't matter what he said; he was repeating himself. I kept thinking *Nope not getting another chance* but I was too tired to argue, so I merely said once again that I would think it over, even though I'd had sufficient time to figure out that I was no longer interested.

A few days later, I found a long note under my door. That scared me.

"I could wear jeans so the date is more casual," it read. *Huh?* I guess my neighbor had repeated my offhand remark about how it had felt too formal. I didn't need a guy in jeans. Back was trying way too hard. He was bending over backwards to please me, and it was creepy.

He didn't live anywhere near me and had come all the way back to my door to leave a note? He was impatient, and he was back. He didn't realize how he was coming across, but I was beginning to feel stalked.

I quickly called my neighbor and told her my decision was a definite hard no. No to dates, no to being put on the spot, no to ultimatums, no to calls, no to notes, no to Back or being jean-stalked. Just no.

A Walk in the Park

I had recently begun to google my dates and it was appalling to see what turned up. My last date was okay, but seemed too smooth and he gave off an undefinable vibe. So, when I got home, I googled him and quickly discovered why. He had been indicted for embezzlement. The *shadchan* had told me he was an attorney. I had not been told he was a disbarred lawyer. When I told him that I had found unflattering things about him online, I was hoping he'd express remorse. As it was not raining men, I tried hard to give him the benefit of the doubt, but he displayed anger.

"Oh, that's the gift that keeps on giving," he snarled. "My rabbi loves me, my kids love me, my community loves me." *Sure, 'cause you gave them gifts from stolen cash?*

Another man whose references I had called, was *still married*. More than ten years after his divorce, he had still not given his wife a *get*. His references had given glowing reviews, "He's our *ben bayis* and so wonderful!"

I had not thought to google him till after our date. *Were they truly in the dark or were they protecting him? He's married!*

I was certainly racking up stories – of dates with crooks and married men – but I was still no closer to getting married. My despair was growing.

One day, I was supposed to meet a friend in the park, on our lunch break. I didn't spot my friend, so I circled around the park, finally gave up, and sat near a fountain. The sound of the water soothed me. The weather was gorgeous, the water glistened. Random jets of water sprayed as kids gingerly stepped in or spread their arms as they ran through in wild abandon. A toddler tipped over when the spray of

180

water was too strong and giggled loudly. Without a thought, I turned to the man on my right eating his lunch.

"Cute, isn't she?"

His eyes widened in surprise at my unexpected remark. He smiled broadly at the shared diversion. That's when I really glanced at him. At that moment I wished that I could have a blind date show up just once with that look of open friendliness and grace on his face. His smile was warm, his teeth so white. He looked way too young, and of course not Jewish and I didn't need this frustration. I turned back to the antics at the fountain.

But he began, "This so nice to watch. Beautiful here in park," he pointed outward with his fork. His English was not perfect but good enough to understand. Then he told me that he missed his wife and kids who lived in South America. He was here working on a visa, trying to save money to send home and that's why he never went out to eat with his colleagues. He brought his home-made lunch to the park. His lunch bag was safely planted on the bench between us like a *mechitzah*. We found out our jobs were closely related and then when I asked where he worked, he said, "A small building on a small street."

I worked in a big building on a big street, but I used to work in a small building in the area. When I pressed him, it turned out he worked in the very same building I had worked at years ago. We were amazed at the odds of that, and spoke for another twenty minutes or so. It was easy, interesting, and despite the language barrier, conversation flowed. But he wasn't Jewish and he was married. I yearned for just such an easy flow of words with a Jewish date. I could feel my heart slowly begin to ache with longing and knew I had to shake it off. I didn't need this heartache. We got up to leave.

"It was nice meeting you," I said, knowing I wouldn't see him again.

"Will you be in the park again?" he asked.

"I don't come here regularly," I said, even though I did. "Well, it was nice meeting you. Have a great day." I was trying to wrap it up and leave.

"You too. You too." Clearly, he had enjoyed the company. He missed his family and had shown me their photos. He was lonely in New York, and just sharing that with me had done something for him.

I did like going to the park, but I avoided it. I didn't want to run into Parkman. Weeks later, I ventured back to a completely different section of this big park. I was reading, watching the tourists, and enjoying the sunshine when suddenly Parkman appeared with a huge smile on his face, "How are you? I've been looking for you for weeks!" *Wow. He didn't give up on me. He had looked for me? Why can't a frum guy ever do something like that? God, You're not making things easy.*

I had just had a date with a *frum* guy who turned out to be an embezzler. Parkman's interest validated me as someone deserving more than that. *God, why do You test me this way?* I didn't want this frustration or this test. But okay, he was friendly. We just talked. It was out in a public park. He kept reminding me he was married, and I reminded him that I was an observant Jew. He put his lunch between us on the bench. So, we had our *mechitzah* and we were in public. What could happen?

I'll tell you what happened. We became friends who looked forward to sharing lunch once a week – and we both felt guilty about it. We never called each other at home or in the office. We never met after work. We never took the bag away from between us. He was growing on me, but I never told him. I was growing on him, and he never told me, but I could tell. We both knew and we both felt guilty. And we both couldn't stop, because he missed his wife and kids terribly, and I was stuck dating embezzlers and men who refused to give their wives a *get*.

We shared childhood stories and compared our cultures, history and lifestyles. We thought we weren't crossing any lines, but if we felt guilty obviously there was a certain comfort level between us that was inappropriate. We knew it.

I prayed to God more than ever to help me find the right person for me. I told God that I had not offered my number or asked for his, that I had not returned to the park, and had avoided it for weeks. I asked *Hashem* for His help. My mind and emotions could barely manage this conflict between the men I could date but did not wish to, and the men

I couldn't date and wished I could. It was an unbearable test – not at all a walk in the park. *Why was I going through this? Why won't You, Hashem, allow me to do the right thing with the right person?* I was losing my mind.

God did help. Though He didn't bring me a man who matched Parkman's grace, open friendliness, and intellect, He did remove the test. Parkman decided to return to his family and his country. I would miss him and remember him fondly, but I was grateful to God.

Talk isn't Cheap at All

Over the years, the challenges I faced drove me to seek help. I had received much unsolicited advice from strangers, ex-dates, matchmakers and acquaintances, when I would've preferred date referrals from them. However, when I sought advice I turned to family, friends, rabbis, rebbetzins, others who had married late, and mentors of all sorts that I trusted. Some people offered practical tips and advice. Others did not.

I'd been constantly working on myself, and after much self-introspection, despite my skepticism, I thought perhaps it's time to engage a professional to help me deal with the conflict and my lost hopes of ever becoming a Jewish wife and mother. My situation was painful, yet I didn't want to become embittered by it. I wanted to learn how to cope with it and fix it. I began to look for a therapist instead of a husband, and soon discovered the task was equally daunting.

Finding a therapist also consisted of asking for recommendations, initial awkward calls, and uncomfortable questions. The therapists would respond to any of my inquiries with "If you book a session, I'll address that when we meet." At $250 a visit, with no idea what their goal or technique would be, I was wary, but decided to give it a shot.

My first try was a *frum* female therapist whose office was in her home basement. It was a cold, snowy day, and she had told me not to arrive late nor early. If I came late, I would be charged for her time, but if I came early, I was not to ring the bell or enter, so the patient she was with could have privacy leaving. Adhering to her instructions, after getting off the bus, I wandered the streets breathing out puffs of air, watching them float into the dark, sensing my fingers turn numb in my gloves, and feeling pathetic for having paid for the honor to freeze outdoors as I circled aimlessly. When it was time, I turned back to her home, rang the bell and she buzzed me in.

"Excuse me a moment, I'm in the middle of renovating my home. I just need to speak to the contractor, I'll be right back," she said. The minutes ticked by as I heard her discuss carpet installations and paint. At over $4 a minute, I was curious if she'd give me the lost time at the end of my slot. I scanned the beautifully furnished office. *Did I just pay for a few cans of paint while twiddling my thumbs here?* Just as my annoyance was growing, she returned with a rueful smile and "Sorry!"

"So," I began, "how exactly does this work? How would you help me?"

"Well for one thing, the first few sessions, I ask the questions, not you." *Ouch.* "We do a background, family bio, and go from there," she said. "It usually takes at least ten sessions to get to solving any issues." *Ten sessions? $2500? That would pay for her carpet, wouldn't it?* I still had no idea what she would offer me or how she would help me. I was uneasy, but I had already committed to this session so I willed myself to bend, not be so stubborn and just try it.

She began, ironically, by grilling me with the very same questions that my dates asked – the questions I intensely disliked. "So how many sisters and brothers do you have?"

I groaned inwardly. *Did the number of siblings I have influence my fate? After all, my siblings had the same number of siblings as I did, and they were married!* I had read about birth order theory and how childhoods affected adults, but she still had not clarified what our path would be or how she would help. I was torn. I wanted to give this a shot, but I already didn't like or trust this woman. I fumbled through the session, feeling violated and in no way relieved. *We had not said one word about why I was there in the first place! Was there something wrong with me for wishing to address that?*

I didn't feel comfortable being interrogated by her. Perhaps this could work, but I needed to find someone I trusted. She urged me to book my next session, but I wouldn't ever freeze my fingers for her again nor finance her home renovations. I moved on.

I found another therapist recommended by a couple who had raved about him. They said he had saved their marriage, so with high hopes I shlepped out to New Jersey for my session. On the phone, he told me he wasn't religious, but had many Orthodox clients and understood our lifestyle. I wasn't keen on discussing my situation with an irreligious Jewish married man, but he was a professional, right?

We had a friendly start, but he too wanted background information. However, he didn't want to start with my family life. He was taking a different tack.

"Why don't you tell me about your sex life?" he asked. *There goes another $250 down the drain.* If he was familiar with religious lifestyles, he wouldn't be asking this question first thing. I was here to discuss dating, communication, my desire to get married and my failure to do so, and within five minutes he chose to veer towards a sex discussion? His line of questioning felt downright voyeuristic and intrusive. He had not earned my trust. I would not discuss that with him. I just wanted to leave and told him so. Next.

I called a *frum*, married, male therapist who had a stellar reputation. I didn't think he'd understand a single woman, but again was willing to try. On the phone he sounded stern and serious and also responded to my questions with "I'll address that in a session." *Ka-ching.* No way. I wasn't doing that again. If he could not invest a few minutes of time in advance, then he was not for me.

I put this all aside. It was clearly not working for me. I was beginning to doubt myself, but I knew my single status did not mean I was inferior nor more troubled than married people. There were plenty of people who were selfish, crazy, angry, depressed, ugly – and still managed to meet their mate. I could not allow my self-esteem to falter.

Months later, I attended a *shiur* in the Five Towns. The lecturer spoke with intelligence and humor and captured her audience's attention easily.

It was only later that I discovered that this mesmerizing speaker was a therapist as well. When I found out, I called her and she offered me a free trial session, so I met with her. She was smart and compassionate, but one glance at her revealed she was clearly in the midst of dealing with a serious illness with apparent grace. Perhaps I could learn something valuable from her. It would certainly put my own troubles in perspective.

Right at the start, I trusted her, felt comfortable with her, and valued her insights. She was very kind. She never let me wait alone at the deserted train station in the dark or cold. She drove me to the station, insisted I wait in her warm car till the train appeared, and didn't charge me for the extra time.

Several things niggled at me on the train ride home. I felt petty talking about myself. She was filled with optimism – despite her illness and treatments – while I felt devoid of hope in the face of a seemingly bleak future despite all my blessings. It seemed all wrong. I felt ashamed to feel despair and unburden myself to this woman just a few years older than myself, who was facing a deadly disease. I could only hope our sessions served as a distraction for her from her own problems rather than an irritation. It was always a quiet, sobering ride back to the city. Each time I disembarked at Atlantic Terminal, the shock of light and noise, and the foul smells that accosted me, jolted me back to the harsh reality of my own wretchedness.

Many of her insights were things that had taken me years to learn. I felt saddened that I hadn't met her earlier when she could've spared me years of figuring it all out on my own. In addition, discussing my situation on a regular basis made me dwell on it more. It was a downer, and it depressed me. I could be the best version of myself and take into account all her tips, but the reality was that the pool and quality of available men had shrunk considerably in my age range while the competition was fierce. Finding a suitable mate was logistically tougher than ever.

She had given me exercises to see whether my expectations were realistic. Over the years, I often noticed that people aspired to others who were way above their own league. The sixty-five-year-old heavy guy with the triple chin and pock-marked face longed to marry the thirty-year-old slim beauty; the uneducated girl wanted to marry the guy with the MBA, and so on. It could happen, but it was a long shot. People could have their unreasonable dreams, but I had long ago turned inward and focused on attaining all the qualities I was looking for, and *becoming* the person I wanted to marry.

In time, she gave me the validation I needed that I was doing everything I could do. I decided to pause on the sessions just as she unfortunately was losing her battle against her disease. I prayed for her daily and it put my own misfortunes in perspective. Eventually, this beautiful, kind, giving soul was taken from this world.

In the end, talk is cheap but it is action that defines a person.

Richie Rich

Some men I met along the way kept up with me sporadically, but if they were *frum* and marriage-minded, they eventually married and we lost touch. I valued friendship wherever I found it and some of my dearest friends were often not my peers. My married friends were occupied with their families or had moved away. My single friends were caring for their parents, or were busy dating. Sometimes the people who had the most time or interest to engage with me were people, whether religious or not, who were at different stages of life than I was. Whether it was someone like GothGuy or a *frum*, older widow with kids learning in *kollel*, I could be friends with anyone if they were open to being friends with me and we had some rapport.

I had once heard a rebbetzin speak about single older women and widows, and the pain we all go through. She acknowledged that the grief for these two cohorts were different. Then she expressed her puzzlement at why gatherings and outings organized for widows attracted more participants than gatherings organized for single women. I could've explained it to her. Widows had been married, had children, and mourned a loss that changed their lives. They needed a support system to fill the ensuing void. They welcomed the chance to meet others in the same situation.

As a single woman for decades, the last thing I needed was a group to help me hang out with other single women. I had been doing that for decades on my own. I was at the stage where I preferred sharing my Shabbos meals with families or a mix of people than a table full of "girls" where the talk naturally would turn to bad dates and relationships.

I didn't want to become a statistic or a bitter old maid. I didn't want to bash men. I wanted to marry one. I preferred meeting people I could engage with or learn from, or men who could help me remember I was a woman.

Richie Rich was one of those men.

I met him online. I suspected he might be a bit too old for me and a bit too modern, but his emails had not scared me away, so I was willing to meet – as everyone repetitively told me, *you never know*. At first glance, I saw he was not wearing a *kippah*, and he looked even older than I thought. It turned out that he claimed to be religious because he occasionally fasted on Yom Kippur, attended Passover Seders, and had a Bar Mitzvah. But he didn't observe Shabbos, keep kosher, or observe Judaism regularly. He had no clue that my level of observance was so much higher than his.

He also turned out to be considerably older than me. *Here we go again: this is just all wrong.* I'd make the most of the dinner, get through it, go home, and put this behind me. Richie Rich was short, balding, and confidently bragged about his money, while telling me he was the least materialistic person he knew. *If you're trying to impress me, you've got the wrong woman.* I was not attracted to wealthy businessmen. I seemed to be more in tune with the philosophical, artistic types. Initially I was turned off as I usually am by such talk, but as he went on, I found much of it amusing and interesting. I had never had the opportunity before to openly question a rich man about his wealth.

"So how many homes do you have? You've already mentioned at least three," I asked, wondering how many homes an unattached man needed and why.

"I've got properties here and there, but really, I'm telling you my house in the Hamptons is the smallest house there. I used to have a four-bedroom home with a pool when I was married, but we never had kids and it's just more stuff to take care of. I never even swam in that pool." *Sigh. I would've enjoyed a pool in the Hamptons.*

"My house is tiny. In fact, most women are upset when they see how small it is. Even my Bel Air house is too small for most women."

"You mean most gold digger women," I said. "Maybe you're just not dating the right type of woman. Didn't you say you have a four-car garage? How small could that house be?"

"The house is smaller than the garage," he said. *Maybe he's lying or bragging, but at least he didn't ask me how many sisters and brothers I had.* He was making me laugh and he also turned the conversation to me and asked about my observance. He seemed intrigued by it. The other non-observant men I had met were usually turned off by religion. Richie Rich was not. He was curious and interested. By the end of the date, I thought *Hey, that wasn't so bad, but he is so not for me.* But Richie Rich asked me out again.

"Why would you want to go out with me again? I'm too religious for you– and, might I add, too young!"

"I don't mind. I like you, so whaddaya say?" *I mind! We have nothing in common!*

I hesitated, so he barreled right along as the wheeler dealer he was, "You don't have to answer now. Sleep on it and we'll email." Of course, after that he emailed and I told him I couldn't date him, but he took it graciously and didn't seem to care. He continued to email me some more, and slowly, but surely, he wormed his way into my life. I didn't understand this. He was friends with people who lived in the Hamptons and partied with celebrities. I didn't run in those circles or dress or act like those people at all.

"Exactly. All the Jewish women I date are Japs, and you're not. That's what I like about you."

"Maybe because you're hanging out in the wrong places like Bel Air, the Upper East Side, and the Hamptons," I said. *Does he schlep his clothes from place to place? Where does his mail go? Who cuts the grass or shovels the snow? How do the wealthy manage all this? Do his car batteries die?* A whirl of questions about this lifestyle aroused my curiosity, so I didn't mind the chance to talk to a guy like this. But I would not date him.

The Very Long Prenup

"You buy double of everything?" I was incredulous.

"Yes, I have the same exact clothes in my NY apartment and my Bel Air home," he said. *Wow.* Then he went on, "So you're sure you don't want to marry me?" I was amazed by his double wardrobe but, no, I would not marry someone because he has the same striped socks on each coast. No.

"Not unless you keep Shabbos and kosher," I teased. But even if he were observant, we weren't compatible and I had made that clear to him several times. We could speak and be friends, but I would move on and date others. I was interested in learning about his jet set lifestyle. I never knew anyone like him. That's all.

Richie Rich was persistent, "I can try to keep Shabbos and kosher," he offered. It was clear he knew so little he wouldn't know how to keep Shabbos. I could teach him regardless, for his own sake, but I still wouldn't marry him. I counter-offered, "That would have to go in our prenup."

"I'm game," he said, and so began our small "prenup" that mushroomed every time we spoke. We had some serious talks about God and Judaism and he asked me to translate a photo of his grandfather's gravestone. He knew he was a *Kohen* but it seemed his grandfather also had been a rabbi. He said his father had never been religious, and his mother had rebelled against her religious parents.

"See? My grandfather was a rabbi! Now you can marry me."

"Not unless you *daven* three times a day with a *minyan*," I retorted. I wouldn't marry him even then. He was much older and we weren't a match in any way.

"Let's put that in the prenup," he said resignedly.

"Okay that goes on page 351," I kidded. This imaginary prenup was getting huge.

I was not interested in him as a potential husband, but I was concerned about him as a human being and as a Jew. He taught me about business and I taught him about *Yiddishkeit*.

I wanted to lease a car, but was afraid of the process. He told me to call him if I had trouble at the dealership. Of course, I had trouble. When I called him, he was at the dentist, but in between gargles he said, "Put that sales guy on the phone." He knew what to say and do and many of the fees on my contract disappeared.

Once or twice a year, we'd go for dinner. One time, we ran into some friends of his and he introduced me by exclaiming, "My friend here keeps Shabbos and kosher!" I could see that he was proud of my observance.

I ignited his Jewish pride, but he went straight back to dating non-Jewish women. I tried to talk him out of that. I didn't want to bombard him or be too pushy with religion, but I was available for all his questions. I sent him YouTubes of cantorial music and he noticed *shiurim* pop up on the side suggestions. He started clicking on those without any prompting from me. One day he excitedly sent me a YouTube of Rabbi Manis Friedman discussing the soul, "Now that's a rabbi I like!" he declared. He was amazed that I had already heard of Rabbi Friedman and said, "If I'd had a rabbi like that *Bar Mitzvah* me, I would probably be observant today." As though "Bar Mitzvah" was a verb and the rabbi could just wave a wand and make him religious.

"You still can be! Rabbi Akiva didn't start learning until he was forty and he became the rabbinic leader of the generation," I said.

"I'm so used to my life. I can't change now," he said. "I'm sorry I'm a terrible Jew."

In a stroke of synchronicity, I had just read a great definition of a good Jew which I repeated to Richie Rich. "A good Jew is a Jew at any level who tries to be a better Jew." I knew religious Jews who didn't truly connect with God or incorporate the essence of Judaism, or those who focused on rituals but neglected ethics or interpersonal niceties. Richie Rich was not observant, but he was kind, generous, and had a *pintele Yid*. He cared about his Jewish soul and was proud of Jews. He wasn't a liberal, secular Jew who was embarrassed by religious Jews. He could be a good Jew if he chose to be. I encouraged him to pick one *mitzvah* to focus on. He asked me which one.

"Why don't you start wearing *tefillin?*" I suggested.

"No way! I don't understand phylacteries at all. I have to do something I understand," he grumbled.

I gave him several *mitzvos* to choose from, and he chose Friday night candle lighting. I bought him crystal candlesticks and he said I was the only one who bought him good gifts: this man had everything he wanted, including houses and cars, but he was getting *Jewish* gifts from me. I had bought him a Yom Kippur *machzor* with an English translation and commentaries. These were things he didn't have, but was clearly interested in.

Then he surprised me "I bet you didn't know that I said *Kaddish* for both of my parents. I only did it once a day, but wherever I was, I found a synagogue whether it was Reform or Chabad, or anything in between. I did it." I was so astonished and pleased that I forgot to ask whether he had done it in Hebrew or English.

So, despite our growing "prenup" of things he didn't do, every Friday night, no matter where he travelled, he began to light the Shabbos candles as Jewish families all over the world did. He delighted in being part of the family.

WomanGirl

One spring morning – the kind where brighter sunlight, fresher air, and emerging blooms fill one up with promise and optimism, I entered the hospital glad to finally be rid of the large protruding fibroid in my belly. It had grown from plum size to peach size and had reached grapefruit size, pressing on my bladder and protruding from one side of my belly. I didn't want to have it grow to watermelon size. I didn't want to look pregnant, especially as I wished I really *were* pregnant; mostly, I wanted to relieve the pressure on my bladder.

Dr. K. told me that he would remove the fibroid only, even though many doctors would insist on hysterectomy for women my age. He understood that I had not delayed motherhood for a career. I was religious. I wanted to marry and have kids.

Hours later, I woke from surgery in the customary fog. In my half-sleep state, I remembered. My fingers roamed over my abdomen to check the staples. They should have been horizontal in a Caesarean-style cut. The doctor assured me that after a laparoscopic check, it would be that way unless something went wrong, and there was only the smallest chance of that happening...

as it did...

The odds were as low as winning the lottery, yet I had managed to "win" this devastating numbers game. While I lay oblivious on the operating table, the pathology report during surgery raised red flags. There were unrecognizable cells. The surgeon made the fateful decision to pre-empt any possibility of the silent killer, otherwise known as ovarian cancer, taking root in my abdomen.

I was dumbfounded. *God, what have You done to me?*

If it's possible to be in a state of shock while not fully conscious, I was. My eyes were still closed as my fingers gingerly traced the trail of staples zippering around my belly button and vertically downward another few inches. They were not horizontal. I heard my sister's voice from afar. My lashes fluttered. Then my doctor's face materialized over mine. I understood what all this meant. He may very well have averted disaster. But I also knew my chances for bearing a child had rapidly gone from "declining" to a very solid "none."

I was horrified. The narrow window of opportunity had slammed shut.

My body that had pained me monthly for decades had failed me. The children who would have made all that pain worthwhile were not to be. The husband I had searched for had not been found on time. A lifetime of longing and prayer has led to this. This slammed door, this soul-crushing slammed door.

Dr. K. hovered above me. "You're going to be alright," I heard him say. He may have saved my life, but in this moment, I loathed him. He appeared blurry through my tears and his words seemed empty and ludicrous. *Alright? He means all wrong!*

"Thank you for saving my life," I dutifully said, feeling my lips move as though someone had pressed my "play" button. A million conflicting thoughts numbed my devastated soul stuck on "stop" and looking for "rewind." The doctor may very well have averted disaster, years of treatment, sorrow, and even death but I despised what he had done. I felt like punching him.

Between waves of awareness and gratitude that a benign fibroid may have averted ovarian cancer, I was furious at God for what He had allowed to happen. What was I supposed to learn from all this? If the fibroid was a miracle from God, the abnormal cells and the resulting infertility were from God as well. The years and years of trying to get married, the dream of having children were like a house of cards that had come tumbling down.

I was a rare and sad anomaly. I was unexpectedly thrust into surgical menopause – as a virgin. Hot flashes replaced cramps. I had lost my womanhood before my girlhood.

What was I? A girl? A woman? A womangirl?

The clock had been ticking, but now it was over. Over and done.

I cried. There was nothing else to do.

And somehow, in time, this poem emerged from my grief.

The Loss without a Marker

Sometimes there is a body, a grave, a stone,
a day - a focal point for grief.
and everyone knows and empathizes.

They grasp for words that can never adequately comfort.
There is an acknowledgement – as obvious as a *shiva* call
or as subtle as an empathetic look, a fleeting touch on the shoulder
or some shared emotion thick in the air
and the griever cries knowing the world listens and cares.

But sometimes a griever's grief creeps upon them
   gradually over years
or with abrupt suddenness

And the grief is private, a whisper in the world
that ebbs and flows with fear and time.
One cannot proclaim it –
Not even when one is sure that fear and time have fled
   leaving grief on its own.

and there is no day, no place, no focal point to mourn
for a husband never found, for children never born,
for wishes and hopes and prayers never fulfilled.

There is no body, no grave, no stone.
And the griever, grieves alone.

The Audacity of Anger

Throughout it all, I always had a relationship with God. When I was angry about my situation, angry at people, at life, at God, I still knew the veracity of Judaism was sound. Sometimes I put all my energy into pleasing Him, studying His Torah, fulfilling His commandments. My soul would feel connected and wished to do everything the way a Jew is supposed to by stretching myself, molding my character, following rituals, and passing ethical tests that cropped up daily.

In times of distress, of course I'd pray to God fervently and hope He heard. When I witnessed seeming injustice – although I understood that there is a bigger picture I cannot see and that justice would prevail in the end – sometimes it left me feeling indignant and angry.

I am human and it is the ultimate human question – why do bad things happen to good people? The question of the book of *Job*.

After the surgery, I returned to *shul* as soon as I was able, but I felt aggrieved and completely deflated as a woman. My body was now scarred, and so was my soul. I hoped my attendance would reignite my spirit, or at least compensate for my inability to pray. I didn't just question God's ways; I had the audacity to be angry at God Himself. I was not very comfortable with that feeling.

I knew I had much to be grateful for, so I made an appointment with a rebbetzin, a mentor, to talk it through. I'd attended her adult classes over the years. She always recharged my spiritual battery and inspired me to want to be a better person and Jew. I regarded her as the epitome of what a religious teacher should be because she practiced what she preached. She was always accessible for questions and never asked for anything in return. I had already discussed my feelings with her when I turned forty. I knew she would be understanding and kind, but I felt more vulnerable than ever. I told her about my surgery and my grief. I told her I was angry at God and then too ashamed to have had the audacity to be angry at Him.

My rebbetzin reassured me, "If you are angry at God, that means you still have a relationship with Him. If you were indifferent, now *that* would be a problem." *Whew*, I thought. *So, I'm not completely lost.*

But I felt very lost.

"I can barely pray when I feel this way."

She looked at me with kindness in her eyes and said, "You are human. It is normal to grieve and to question. If you cannot use the prayer book, pray from your heart. Talk to Him directly. Tell Him what you feel."

With one brilliant stroke she absolved me of the burden of guilt. She reassured me that faith is often coupled with doubt, and that it was okay. She gave me an alternate way to speak to God till this anger would pass. She gave me a way to carry on.

I carried on.

The Phone Call

I carried on, but I struggled. At this stage, my dreams of motherhood were elusive. Perhaps I'd be a stepmother or adopt a child, but it seemed unlikelier than ever. I had spent an enormous amount of time and effort trying to become a Jewish wife and mother. I had that role instilled in me by my schooling, my society, and my own desire, however by God's design and my missteps I had never achieved that goal. *What did God want from me? Was the ultimate mission to be a Jewish wife and mother? If so, what was my mission now?* I would need to re-evaluate my purpose on this planet and recalibrate.

I doubted the power of prayer. Yes, it was very nice that Sarah, our foremother, prayed for a child, but I was fairly certain that I myself would not have a child at ninety years of age, no matter how hard I prayed. I would not even *want* a miracle like that at that age. It already felt too late at this stage. Sarah, Rachel and Chana were "remembered" on Rosh Hashanah and granted children.

But there were many others – even great, pious rabbis and their wives – who were denied children. Were their prayers meritless? Were mine half-worthy or even heard at all?

I had learned that no prayer was ever in vain or unanswered. Perhaps in place of what was intended, another blessing was received. But I was a grieving woman with no clear answers.

One Shabbos morning, I sat with my prayerbook in my lap unable to pray – it felt completely futile. I stared at the words on the page without seeing them and could not say them. I shut the *siddur* and placed it back on the shelf. The words on the page did not express what I was feeling. I could not pray from my heart, as I had been advised, either. God knew how much I'd tried and how much I'd cried. I hoped He understood.

Sunday morning, I felt miserable for not having prayed on Shabbos. I pulled the *siddur* off the shelf again, determined to pray this time. I knew the world was unfair and that I could not see the big picture. I knew I had plenty to be grateful for, but I still didn't want to be one voice in a community of voices. I wanted to stand out and be heard. *I want a one-on-one with You, God.*

This time, I heeded the advice and I prayed from my heart. I stared at the light fixture, the way I gaze at my candles Friday night, as though God is in the light. It somehow seemed appropriate to look up there. *Where are You?* I knew God was everywhere. I talked to Him: *God, I've prayed to you for years and years begging for a spouse, for a family. Perhaps the answer is "No." Perhaps there is a reason why I'm still alone. But how do I know that You're listening to me or hearing me at all?*

I looked away from the ceiling, feeling absurd. I rocked gently in my recliner, my *siddur* open, flat on my lap. I closed it. *Please give me a sign that You've heard me, even if Your answer is "No." I beg You, give me a sign so that I know.*

I leaned my head back, closed my eyes, and sighed from the intensity of my efforts. The phone rang and startled me.

Ha. That must be God. What is He going to sound like? I thought, knowing it can't possibly be Him. *Or could it?* I had goosebumps. I didn't recognize the phone number. I didn't feel like talking to anyone, but if I didn't answer the phone, I'd always wonder who it was.

Ring a ling a ling. My heart jumped at the sound. I grabbed the phone.

"Hello?"

"I'm calling from the charity for…"

My heart sank. What had I been hoping for? I cut her off, "I never pledge over the phone. You can send an envelope my way…." I was in no mood for this sort of call, and I truly never pledged for fear I would forget.

"I'm not calling for a pledge. I'm calling to let you know you won our Chinese auction and should be getting your prize in the mail soon."

"I won?" *I've never won anything in my life.* I looked up at the ceiling again, trying to recall which auction this was.

"Yes, you won a tri-color gold necklace and bracelet set. Please let us know if it does not arrive in a few days." It did arrive, and was beautiful and dainty with little white, yellow, and red gold beads.

Was the call coincidence? Divine Providence? I had begged God to give me a sign and the phone rang. I call it my "God-is-Listening" jewelry, and I wear it when I need God close to me.

Kadosh

I had not told my father the specifics of my surgery. I had tested the waters earlier by mentioning that I needed surgery, and he rebuffed me, "No, you don't need surgery." I had to explain my absence, so that he wouldn't be alarmed when I didn't answer his calls, but quickly realized I would not be able to share details with him. So, after the surgery, while aggrieved about my situation, I faked being okay whenever I was with him. It was my siblings who lent me their ears and shoulders.

I vacillated between hope in God and feeling completely abandoned, between feeling strong, and feeling vulnerable. I should not have dated anyone at this time, but I did, and I messed it up. I talked too much. I cried. After years of restraint, I once again slipped in my resolve to be *shomer negiah* and slipped my hand in his. The momentary pleasure of a man's embrace was not worth the disappointment that followed. I felt like I had let down my guard and let down my God, and even let down my date. It wasn't the way I wanted to behave and I don't think it was the way he wanted to behave either. Neither of us were casual touchers, and yet it had happened. *Selach li. Forgive me.* My fault. I hoped my mother wasn't disappointed in me up in *Gan Eden.*

Despite unfulfilled needs, I didn't want random encounters. I wanted a deep and meaningful commitment before touching someone. I wanted what my married friends had and what I had been working tirelessly towards. I had learned that *kadosh,* which means holy, was the same root of the two words *kedushin* and *kedeisha,* respectively meaning marriage and prostitute. The sex act is the same for both, but the fine line between the two was commitment. Marriage according to Jewish law signifies the commitment between two partners and that is what makes the same act truly holy – *kadosh* – in the eyes of God. At my core, my soul yearned and needed for my physical acts to be *kadosh.*

Loss Upon Loss

Richie Rich called me excitedly from his winter home on the West Coast to tell me he was "off the market." In his characteristic way, he used business terminology to tell me he was engaged. I couldn't have been more surprised. Aside from the fact that I thought he was too stuck in his ways to marry again so many years after his divorce, his fiancée was much younger, and not Jewish. After all his learning, interest in Judaism, and growing appreciation of it, I had wished that if he ever would marry, it would be to someone with similar Jewish values who was closer to his own age. I hoped this woman wasn't another gold digger. He was much wiser when it came to business than women.

He knew I wasn't thrilled, so he argued defensively that he wanted to marry a Jewish woman, but "Jewish women are all Japs!"

"Hey, I'm not!"

"You don't count. You're not the type of woman I'm talking about! Besides, you didn't want to marry me even with a 3,000-page prenup." *That's true.*

I told him that as a friend who understood loneliness all too well, I was glad he found companionship, but as a religious Jew I could not support his choice. He was disheartened more than angry.

"I'm not telling you how to live your life," I said, "I'm just telling you what the law is – giving you the information. I do want you to be happy. It's not like I'm telling you to stay alone while I'm happily married. You know that I'm also on my own and paying a price for it."

"Yeah, I know you're the real deal. No doubt about that." Richie Rich knew about my difficulties. Once when we met for dinner, he asked about my latest dates. I admitted I hadn't had one in nearly a year. He was astounded and aggravated, and immediately whipped out his cellphone and called his religious accountant to see if he knew anyone for me.

"But it's not like I'm going to have kids anymore," he said as though that were the main issue. We rehashed some of the arguments we had about his dating life.

"I'll convert her," he offered. "My ex converted."

"It doesn't work that way. It wouldn't be a kosher conversion as I'm sure your ex's wasn't. Besides if it *were* a kosher conversion, you wouldn't be able to marry her anyhow."

"Whaddaya mean? Why not?"

"Because you're a *Kohen*." Richie Rich had known he was a descendant of Moses' brother, Aaron and the *Kohanim*. I had seen a photo of his grandfather's tombstone which confirmed it. There are Jewish laws regarding marriage specifically for *Kohanim*.

"I can't marry her cause she's not Jewish, but even if she does convert, I still can't marry her?"

"That's right."

"So, I'm damned if I do and damned if I don't?"

"Well…you're not damned, but you can't do either. That's right."

Richie Rich was frustrated. He wanted to do the right thing, but all these rules bewildered him. While he was engaged to this non-Jewish woman, he continued to read articles on intermarriage, trying to find loopholes for himself while listening to online rabbinical lectures.

He had watched another YouTube video by Rabbi Friedman on what happens to a Jewish soul after death. He asked me questions about burial. He didn't like the thought of being buried in the ground. "I don't like the idea of worms crawling on me. Makes me squeamish." He had bought a slot in a mausoleum. "I'll have to reconsider that." He had never known the Jewish laws on burial. I thought it was interesting how he was engaged to a gentile woman yet continued to explore Judaism online as well as review his burial plans.

A couple of weeks later he called. "You'll be very pleased to hear that I'm on the market again!" He knew I wasn't thrilled about his engagement, but I was surprised all over again.

"She was a gold digger. She was a liar. How can I marry someone like that?"

I let him talk it out. I knew the pain of breakups all too well.

Two weeks later, I got another call from him. "You know how I told you I took her to a Passover Seder? I got a bad stomachache after that, and I thought it was all the matzoh I ate, but it's an ulcer." I felt bad for him – broken dream and an ulcer.

A couple of weeks later, things worsened. "They misdiagnosed me. It's pancreatic cancer."

Oh, oh. He had gone from seventh heaven to hell very fast. I recalled our recent talks about the soul, the afterlife, and burials – subjects we had discussed before he ever got sick. Things happened rapidly after that. He was hospitalized in Cedars Sinai in LA and I reached the Orthodox chaplain and sent him to Richie Rich. He said Richie Rich had requested candles, *challah* and wine for Shabbos, though he could barely eat a thing.

He was discharged from the hospital. I flew out west to visit him and was alarmed to see how thin and weak he had become. He had a private nurse. He told me he was switching doctors and the new one had told him that without treatment he had eight months left, and with treatment he had more.

All I could think was how swiftly a man's fortune could change for the good or the bad. I flew home wondering if that was the last time I would ever see him.

A week or two later, my father stepped onto a city bus. The driver lurched away from the curb before my father sat down. He fell and broke his hip. I texted Richie Rich: "Now I have to worry about both of you!"

"Just worry about your dad," he texted back.

That same week, I got another text from him. But it was not him. It was his nurse letting me know he had passed. I reread it again and again. *That can't be right.*

He didn't get the promised eight months. He didn't even get one month. I knew he was very ill, but this was a jolt to my system. I doubted that he had changed his burial plans so soon, but his soul had changed. I had impacted him as much as he had impacted me. That much I knew.

At the same time, my father who had successful hip surgery and should've been bound to physical therapy was suddenly on a respirator. Events were spinning out of control.

For the next six months, my father's condition deteriorated. He couldn't talk, walk, or eat. He laid there and suffered. My siblings and I once again scrambled with doctors, rabbis, calls, treatments, diagnosis. We felt helpless through it all. He had already suffered through labor camps, cattle cars, starvation, death marches and more throughout World War II, why did he have to suffer more? All we could do was hold his hand and sing to him. Then after months of torment, he too slipped away to the next world. It felt like the end of an era. Losing a second parent, makes one's own mortality more absolute.

Seeing two strong, vibrant, independent men suddenly wither away and die not long after my fertility had been ripped from me left a void only filled by God's grace.

Spiral

I was fumbling along in my grief, unsure of myself. I had always wanted to be a Jewish wife and mother. Though *frum* Jewish society may make it appear that our mission is to marry and have kids, to learn Torah, settle Israel and more – these are great tools to fulfill our mission, but not our ultimate purpose. It took much contemplation, as well as classes, prayers, discussions with my mentor – along with experiencing the vicissitudes of life – to learn that we really all do have the same mission.

It is to connect with God and try to emulate God, to mold ourselves continually in His ways, no matter what circumstance we find ourselves in. Our mission is to bring Godliness to Earth, to be a "light unto the nations." Whether we find ourselves in poverty, in illness, in Auschwitz, whether through any trials or tribulations, or whether through religious freedom and financial fortune – do we connect to God, emulate Him, make Him known?

It was a new reality to realign my thought processes and learn to make peace with circumstances I couldn't control. I had imagined my grandfather being at my wedding. When he died, I was consoled by the thoughts my parents would be there. But then I lost my mother and had to readjust my reality again. When I watched my nieces and nephews (who had not been born till years after I had started dating) get married, I had to reorient yet again. I would have to surrender to reality rather than cling to what *should-have-been* to survive it.

We too often compare ourselves to those who are more fortunate than us and express envy, when we should compare ourselves to those less fortunate and express gratitude. Easier said than done.

I would circle from strength and belief and prayer, then crumble under the weight of despair, anguish, and defeat. I felt my faith was not consistent. I was going in endless cycles like a hamster on its wheel. I told my Torah teacher how I felt. She responded with her characteristic brilliance, "You are not going in circles. In truth, it is a spiral."

She explained that we are all doing the spiritual work we are here for, contending with God and working our way towards a greater awareness of God's role in our lives.

"With every circle of doubt and faith, you are being tested. You are changing, growing, improving, and fulfilling your mission of figuring it all out."

I wasn't sure whether my spiral was going upwards or downwards and it didn't remove my existential pain, but the thought made sense, assuaged my worries, and gave the pain a purpose. This was not a meaningless circle; this was a spiral with direction. We are *Bnei Yisrael* – the Children of Israel. Yaakov was renamed Yisrael when he struggled with the angel, and Yisrael literally means "struggle." We are the children of struggle. This unending spiral was my struggle.

Ever After

At every single twist and turn, I struggle, fall, pull myself up again. I've come to realize that I cannot choose my fate, but I can choose how I react to it. I can choose to let it control me. I can choose to be enraged by it, bitter over it, make peace with it. I can choose to fight it and try to change it. I can choose to give up. I can choose to get up once more. I can choose my ever after.

Most of us crave love based on companionship, shared experiences, and values, along with romance as a cherry on top. The ultimate love is that embrace between happy spouses. But love comes in many languages. If I am denied one sort of love, shall I fade like a wilted rose and deny myself all love? Shall I allow thorns to prick me and hold me back? Or shall I stop to smell the roses along the way? Shall I work at trying to find other languages of love wherever they may be – starting with loving God and learning to love myself and be good to myself, to others, to children, to animals, to causes?

I hope and pray that all of us who are on our own will have God bless us and fulfill our wishes very soon. God is in charge. "*Imo Anochi batzara*," (Psalms 91:15). God is with us in our distress. He watches us in our struggles. He cries with us when we cry, and cheers us on when we get up again.

Most of all, God loves us.

I do not think of this as the "end." It is not easy, but every day is a new beginning. We all get to fill in the blank.

We are stronger than we think. We come from a chain of strong women starting with our own mothers and grandmothers, going all the way back to our biblical foremothers and all the ordinary Jewish women throughout history who faced extraordinary challenges and met them with bravery and faith.

Perhaps wider society ridicules and casts us as pathetic. Perhaps those who are happily married would never choose to trade places with us. But we are ordinary women doing something very extraordinary. Each time we put our faith before ourselves, each time we hold on to God rather than turn away, we are erecting another spiritual brick, one upon another and building a spiritual skyscraper unequalled by any of the wonders of the world.

We are unmatched. We are strong. This is our challenge, and we will meet it.

Let's choose our language wisely.

"And she lived _____ ever after."

Acknowledgments

WRITING is very much a solitary endeavor, but publishing a book is a team effort. So let me begin at the start. This book was stuck in my head for ages and despite numerous efforts, the perfect words would float off somewhere between my brain and the pen in my hand. After many hours and many attempts, all I had to show for it, was a pile of scribbled, crumpled balls of paper.

Algonquin Jones dared me to a writing challenge of over 1500 words a day for a month. I thought that was beyond me but he said he'd done it numerous times. Well, if this young man had done it, I could try. He taught me to move forward and get words down instead of looking back to perfect page one again and again. With that lesson, the book that had lain dormant in my mind for years was jumpstarted – solid words, good and bad, finally appeared. With the torrent that followed, I quickly switched from pen to keyboard. Without that lesson and challenge, AJ, this would still be an unwritten idea lodged firmly in my mind, so for that, I thank you.

As my manuscript grew, I wrote whenever I had the chance. There were days when I felt my story was worthwhile and other days when I doubted myself. People would see me on my lunchbreak or after work and ask me what I was doing. I shared some chapters and they'd say nice things. But it was difficult to make myself vulnerable and the manuscript grew into a massive mess.

As the book took shape, I often considered trashing the entire thing. I asked readers for feedback and critiques. My readers were different demographics, single, married, divorced, older, younger, female, male, right wing, traditional, Jewish and not. All your thoughtful comments, perspectives, insights and enthusiasm kept me going. It made me realize this was a worthier endeavor than I originally thought and infused me with the confidence to push the book forward to its final form.

Rivy, it was your interest in this project that finally made my doubts take a back seat to my confidence. Your unending enthusiasm for and observations on my manuscript throughout your own major life changes never dimmed. Shifra, you took time out of your busy schedule to comb through the text meticulously and offer critiques. Jack, you patiently answered all my questions. Avigail, you were piqued by the idea of the book before you ever read one word and your support grew with every word you read. To Faige, Steve, JK and others who eagerly read a chapter or two here or there, you all supported my efforts. Thank you all for your confidence and belief in me, for the errors you caught, the insights you offered and mostly for giving me the friendship and encouragement I needed along the way.

When I seriously considered publishing this, I turned to an editor I had worked with on much smaller pieces and apprehensively asked if she would take this project on. I had never worked on a book before and wasn't sure how she would receive it. Charlotte not only took it on between all her other books and a time-consuming, life-changing *Aliyah* but was a masterful editor. She guided me, taught me, cheered me, boosted my flagging courage and more. What began as an unwieldly mess of words was finessed into a polished book. It took nearly four years from the day I wrote my first words in the writing challenge to when I could say "It's a real book!" Thank you, Charlotte, I cannot imagine doing this with anyone but you.

Thank you to my Rebbetzin, a sincere, generous and humble soul who props me up when my spirit wanes. Your wise words strengthen my faith when I most need it. You teach, inspire and advise so many and yet when I reach out for help, you are there as though I am the only student that matters. Thank you.

Thank you to all the warm sincere friends, rabbis, matchmakers and others who took the time to set me up. So much of your time and work goes unrewarded but your efforts and kindness are remembered with gratitude.

To all the men who are part of my story, I like to believe that nothing is in vain. I hope we added something valuable to each other's lives. My prayer is that if you are still unmatched as I am, that God will be busy with miracles in the coming year for us all.

Thank you to all my friends, who take the time to be there for me, lend a shoulder, and make sure I know I matter, you sustain me. I can only hope I'm that for all of you too. Thank you so much.

To my siblings and their families, who would I be without all of you? You are my past, my present and my future. We share our history, joys and sorrows. May we continue to share only blessed occasions and make our dear parents, z"l, proud. Though we have trouble with love in any language, I think I'll be brave. It's just three little words. I love you.

And finally, to God, ever present in my life. Any thanks to You are inadequate. Thank You for the many unseen miracles sent my way, that helped this book happen.

Glossary of Hebrew and Yiddish terms

Adine	Gentle, delicate
Aliyah	The immigration of Jews to Israel; moving to Israel
Avel	Mourner
Ayin hora	Evil eye
Baal teshuvah, baalei teshuvah (pl.)	Literally "those who return." Refers to unaffiliated who become religious
Bachur	Bachelor, but implies "boy"
Baruch Hashem	Thank God
Basherte	Destined one
Bas Yisroel	Daughter of Israel
Ben bayis	Literally "son of the house." Refers to a frequent guest
Bentch	To say Grace after Meals
Besulah	Virgin, maiden
Bikur Cholim	Society that aids the ill. A Bikur Cholim apartment is a temporary residence available to the family of a hospitalized patient
Birchas Hamazon	Grace after Meals
Bitul zman	Literally "squandering time." Refers to time that could otherwise be used for Torah study
Bnos	Sabbath afternoon girl groups
Borei pri ha'adamah	Blessing over vegetables
Brachos	Blessings
Challah	Braided Sabbath bread

Chametz	Leavened bread normally burned or sold to a gentile via a rabbi agent before Passover
Chassidic/Chassidim	A member(s) of a sect founded in Poland in the 18th century by the Baal Shem-Tov and characterized by its emphasis on mysticism, prayer, ritual strictness, religious zeal, and joy. Numerous Chassidic sects have evolved
Chazal	Acronym for "Chachameinu Zichronam Liv'racha" that refers to all sages of the Mishnah, Talmud, and other rabbinic commentators (and their authoritative opinion) from the times of the Second Temple of Jerusalem until the 6th century CE
Cheder	Jewish school for children
Chesed	Acts of loving kindness; can also mean disgrace or abomination
Cholent	Stew served on the Sabbath, prepared the day before and kept warm until the Sabbath day meal
Chosson	Groom
Chumash	Five Books of Moses
Chuppah, chuppos	Marriage canop(y) (ies)
Chutzpah	Audacity, nerve
Daven(ing)(ed)	Pray(ing)(ed)
Derech Eretz Kadma L'Torah	Common courtesy precedes Torah
Emunah	Faith, belief
FFB	Acronym for "frum from birth"
Frum	Observant
Frummed out	Colloquial expression meaning that someone opted for extreme observance
Gai shoyn shlufen	Go sleep already! Go to bed!
Gam zu l'tovah	This too is for the good. Expression used to always see the good in any event
Gan Eden	Garden of Eden
Ger (m.)/giyoret (f.)	Convert
Geshmak	Tasty, delicious

Get	A Jewish legal divorce
Halachos/halachically	Jewish laws/according to Jewish law
Halleluka	Hallelujah (literally: Praise God)
Hamotzi	The blessing over bread
Hashem	God
Hashgachah Pratis	Divine Providence
Hashkafah	Religious outlook
Havdalah	Literally "separation." The ritual marking the end of Sabbath
Hishtadlus	Effort
Hodu L'Hashem	Thanks to God
Ich hob dir lib	I love you
Im Yirtze Hashem	God willing
Imahos	Biblical mothers of the Jewish nation: Sarah, Rebecca, Leah and Rachel
Iyov	Job (from the Book of Job)
Kaddish	Mourner's prayer
Kadosh	Holy
Kashrus	Laws or status of kosher food
K'das Moshe v'Yisroel	According to the laws of Moses and Israel
Kedeisha	Prostitute
Kedushin	The marriage blessings
Kiddush	blessing over wine at Sabbath meals
Kippah, kippot	Skullcap(s), yarmulke(s)
Kiruv	Literally: to bring close. Refers to teaching unaffiliated Jews about Judaism
Kohen	Male descendent of Aron the High Priest from the tribe of Levi
Kohen Gadol	The High Priest in the Holy Temple of Jerusalem
Kollel	An institute of full-time Talmud study for married men
Kugel	A type of quiche prepared before the Sabbath and kept warm till Sabbath day meal

Kumzitz	From the Yiddish "Kum, zitz" ("Come, sit"), a relaxed gathering around a bonfire
Lo tov hayos haadam levado	It is not good that man be alone. (Genesis 2:18)
Lashon hora	Literally "evil tongue." Derogatory speech about a person
Machmir	Stringent in observance
Machzor	Holiday prayer book
Mazel	Destiny, fortune
Mazel Tov	Congratulations
Mechitzah	Synagogue partition between men and women
Mekubal(im)	Kabbalist(s)
Melave Malka	Literally "escorting the Queen." The meal after the Sabbath that figuratively escorts the Sabbath out
Mezuzah	Encased scroll fixed onto doorposts, containing the first two paragraphs of Shema prayer ("Hear O Israel, the Lord our God, the Lord is One.")
Minyan(im)	Prayer quorum(s)
Mishnah	The written collection of oral laws compiled c.200 CE by Rabbi Judah HaNasi. It forms the basic text of the Talmud
Mitzvah, mitzvos	Divine commandment(s)
Moshav	Israeli cooperative settlement that offers more privacy than a communal kibbutz
Moshe	Moses
Na'ase v'nishma	"We will do and we will hear." Proclamation of the Children of Israel at Mount Sinai. (Exodus 24:7) Some translate the expression "We will do and we will obey."
Nachas	Pride and joy, usually in reference to producing grandchildren
Nebechdik	Pathetic
Parshah	Subdivision of the Torah read weekly
Perek Shira	A mystical prayer about creation

Pintele Yid	Literally "a dot of a Jew." Referring to the ever-present Jewish soul even in one estranged from Judaism
Pletzl	Literally "little place." Refers to the Jewish quarter of Paris
Ptcha	A classic Ashkenazic dish made from jellied calves' bones
Rebbe (Lubavitcher)	The leader of the Lubavitch Chassidic sect
Rebbetzin	A rabbi's wife, teacher
Sadducee	A sect that departed from mainstream Jewish beliefs and practices during the era of the Second Holy Temple
Satmar	A Chassidic sect
Segulah, segulos	Action(s) that will remedy or protect one's destiny for the better
Selach li	Forgive me
Seudah	Festive meal
Shabbos(im)	The Jewish Sabbath(s)
Shabbaton(im)	Group gathering(s) that take place over Sabbath
Shadchan(im)	Matchmaker(s)
Shalach manos	Food baskets given out on Purim
Shalom	Hello, peace
Shema	A classic prayer said every morning and before going to bed
Shidduch	Match
Shir Hashirim	King Solomon's Song of Songs
Shiur(im)	Torah lecture(s)
Shiva	Week of mourning
Shiva Asar b'Tammuz	17th day of Hebrew month of Tammuz – fast day that commemorates the breaching of the walls of Jerusalem prior to its destruction
Shmattehs	Rags, clothes
Shomer negiah	Literally "observant of touch." Refers to Jewish restriction on touching those of the opposite sex

Shul	Synagogue
Siddur	Prayer book
Simcha	A happy occasion
Simchas Torah	Annual holiday celebrating the completion of a reading cycle of the Torah
Szeretlek	(Hungarian) I love you
Talmud	Compilation of Mishnah with commentary, the Oral Torah
Talmud Torah	After school classes in Judaism for public school children
Tanach	Acronym representing Bible, Prophets, Writings
Tante	Aunt
Tefillin	Phylacteries
Tehillim	Psalms
Tisha b'Av	Ninth day of the Hebrew month of Av – fast day commemorating the destruction of the first and second Temples
Torah	Bible (specifically the Five Books of Moses)
Tzedakah	Literally "justice," means charity
Tzitzis	Ritual strings hanging on four corners of a man's garment
Yaakov	Jacob
Yeshiva	Jewish school where Torah subjects are taught
Yeshivish	Having the Jewish observances and cultural outlook of the yeshiva world
Yiddishkeit	Jewish way of life
Yisrael	Israel
Yomim Tovim	Jewish holidays
Yonah	Jonah (Jewish prophet)
Yosef	Joseph
Z"l	Acronym for zichrono/a/am l'vracha: of blessed memory; or may his/her/their memory be a blessing

Made in United States
Orlando, FL
24 September 2024

51937117R00136